D0560405

New Perspectives on Psychotherapy
of the Borderline Adult

New Perspectives on Psychotherapy of the Borderline Adult

Edited by

James F. Masterson, M.D.

With contributions by

Peter L. Giovacchini, M.D.

Otto F. Kernberg, M.D.

James F. Masterson, M.D.

Harold F. Searles, M.D.

BRUNNER/MAZEL, *Publishers* • New York

Library of Congress Cataloging in Publication Data

Main entry under title:
New perspectives on psychotherapy of the borderline adult.

Papers presented at a conference held at Hunter College. New York,
Nov. 5, 1977, and sponsored by the Masterson Group.

Includes bibliographies and index.

1. Pseudoneurotic schizophrenia—Congresses. I. Masterson, James F.
II. Masterson Group. [DNLM: 1. Psychotherapy—In adulthood—
Congresses. WM420 bN532 1977]
RC514.N48   616.8'982   77-94736
ISBN 0-87630-175-8

Published by
BRUNNER/MAZEL, INC.
19 Union Square West
New York, New York 10003

MANUFACTURED IN THE UNITED STATES OF AMERICA

Preface

The conference presented in this volume was sponsored by The Masterson Group for the Study and Treatment of the Character Disorders (Adolescent and Adult). The Masterson Group, organized in February 1977, has three functions: teaching, research and treatment. It has a special interest in long-term continuous psychotherapy—a therapeutic need of these patients which is currently grossly neglected because of the emphasis by third-party payers (government and insurance companies) on short-term care.

I would like to acknowledge the vital contributions of the following members of The Masterson Group to the success of the conference: my associate director, William V. Lulow, M.D., Mrs. Nancy A. Scanlan, who bore such a large burden so well, Mrs. Kalia Lulow for her expertise in graphics, and, finally, Mr. Alexander Epting, Jacinta Costello, M.S.W., and Joan Stearns, M.S.W.

JAMES F. MASTERSON, M.D.
Director, The Masterson Group

Contents

Preface v

Introduction ix

1. THE PSYCHOANALYTIC TREATMENT OF THE
   ALIENATED PATIENT 1
   by *Peter L. Giovacchini, M.D.*

   Discussion 20

2. PSYCHOANALYTIC THERAPY WITH THE BORDERLINE
   ADULT: SOME PRINCIPLES CONCERNING TECHNIQUE 41
   by *Harold F. Searles, M.D.*

   Discussion 66

3. CONTRASTING APPROACHES TO THE PSYCHOTHERAPY OF
   BORDERLINE CONDITIONS 75
   by *Otto F. Kernberg, M.D.*

   Discussion 105

4. THE BORDERLINE ADULT: TRANSFERENCE ACTING-
   OUT AND WORKING-THROUGH 121
   by *James F. Masterson, M.D.*

   Discussion 148

   Index 163

Introduction

In the last few years a knowledge explosion has occurred in the concept of the borderline syndrome as a result of parallel breakthroughs in several areas. Psychoanalytic psychotherapy with adults and adolescents under the influence of object relations and ego-psychology theories, as well as research on normal development through direct child observation, has contributed to this progress and led to a more refined understanding of what is wrong—and to the development of more appropriate and effective therapeutic techniques. Widespread therapeutic pessimism has given way to cautious optimism.

The greatest current need in the field has shifted from research to teaching the findings to those who will make the best use of them—psychotherapists working with patients. With this end in mind, The Masterson Group sponsored the conference on New Perspectives on Psychotherapy of the Borderline Adult in November, 1977. However, it is difficult to absorb and integrate complex abstractions after hearing them only once. Consequently, we decided to make the papers available for reflection and study in this volume.

Each of the authors has an outstanding record of achievement. They are all Professors of Psychiatry, Editors of Journals and authors of many papers, as well as books, which have become milestones in the field. Each comes to the area of the borderline syndrome from his own area of professional development and with his own unique and specific perspective. Dr. Giovacchini comes from his interest in psychoanalysis of the character disorders, Dr. Searles from psychoanalytic work with schizophrenics, Dr. Kernberg from psychoanalytic work with adults and adolescents, with emphasis on object relations and ego psychology theories, and Dr. Masterson from psychoanalytic psychotherapy of adolescents and adults with emphasis on object relations and ego psychology theories as viewed from a developmental perspective.

The papers in this volume are not simply the product of accomplished people turning their talents to a temporary recent interest. Rather they are the latest and most recent evidence of the long and continuous struggle each of the authors has undertaken to master this subject, as well as of the deep personal commitment each feels toward his patients. Consequently, the individual perspectives are hard-won and of great value to us all.

The purpose of the conference was to get at the truth—not Giovacchini's truth, nor Searles' truth, nor Kernberg's, nor Masterson's—but *the* truth, as revealed in the exchange of ideas among these experts. The vehicle was for each author's paper to be discussed by the other three authors.

Dr. Giovacchini's chapter on "Psychoanalytic Treatment of the Alienated Patient" presents a detailed case illustration of a borderline woman's use of externalization as a defense mechanism and the therapeutic techniques necessary to deal with that defense. He then discusses some of the adaptations and defenses of the narcissistic disorder, the state of "becoming" as a defensive life-style, and his views on psychoanalysis of the character disorders.

Dr. Searles' chapter on "Psychoanalytic Therapy with the Borderline Adult: Some Principles Concerning Technique" first presents his definition of the borderline (which is later questioned in the discussion by both Kernberg and Masterson) as a patient whose ego functioning is predominantly autistic and whose sense of reality, both inner and outer, is flawed. He then deals with a number of questions concerning therapy with these patients, including: Why must the analyst resist the temptation to impose his reality on the patient? Why can't transference interpretations be used early? Why does the analyst have to learn to be comfortable with the patient's projections? Why must the analyst be cautious regarding premature interpretations of projections? He deals not only with the various kinds of silence that occur, but also with the importance of phraseology and tone. Finally, he discusses why the analyst must be aware of the aspects of his own personality that the patient seizes on as targets for his projections, as well as what projections the analyst's countertransference may cause him to put on the patient.

Dr. Kernberg's chapter on "Contrasting Approaches to the Psychotherapy of Borderline Conditions" outlines a theory of psychoanalytic psychotherapy, summarizes his own approach to borderline patients within this theoretical frame and then examines critically some alternative psychoanalytic psychotherapeutic approaches to borderline conditions. He addresses such questions as: What constitutes psychoanalytic psycho-therapy? Why is classical psychoanalytic instinctual theory inappropriate for borderline patients? How do object rela-tions and ego psychology theories apply with these patients? Why must the analyst maintain a position of technical neu-trality? What are the parameters necessary to assist the pa-tient's functioning? Why and how do clarification and inter-pretation of the transference become the central elements in treatment? What characterizes the British object relations school's approach to treatment? What are the objections to manipulative approaches? He concludes with a case illustrat-ing transference developments in the psychoanalytic psycho-therapy of a borderline patient.

My own chapter on "The Borderline Adult: Transference Acting-Out and Working-Through" describes how the intra-psychic structure of the borderline personality (split object relations unit, split ego) evolves from the separation-indi-viduation failure and later becomes manifest in psychotherapy in various forms of transference acting-out. It then explains why, and demonstrates, through a case illustration, how the therapeutic techniques of confrontation and interpretation deal with the acting-out and provide the necessary framework to allow the patient to work through his conflicts. It addresses such questions as: What therapeutic techniques are necessary for intensive psychoanalytic psychotherapy? What seems to be the most common error in therapeutic technique? How can this be remedied? What were Freud's views on acting-out? How does an understanding of intrapsychic structure help the analyst to understand transference? What is the relation-ship of transference acting-out to working-through? What are the clinical indications to shift from confrontation to interpretation?

The value of the papers themselves was highlighted and the differences between the various authors' points of view were sharpened by the discussions that followed each paper and which have been included in this volume. For example, Drs. Kernberg and Masterson disagreed with Dr. Searles' definition of the borderline and with Dr. Giovacchini's concept of character disorder; Dr. Masterson disagreed with Dr. Giovacchini's concept of limit-setting interventions; and Dr. Searles felt Dr. Masterson's consideration of countertransference was inadequate. These and many other issues are covered in the stimulating discussions.

JAMES F. MASTERSON

New Perspectives on Psychotherapy
of the Borderline Adult

Chapter 1

The Psychoanalytic

Treatment of the

Alienated Patient

Peter L. Giovacchini, M.D.

Many clinicians find the group of patients I am about to discuss intriguing because of the wide gap which may exist between their ability to function and the extent of their structural defects. In contrast to what might be expressed, some of the most primitively oriented characters have been able to achieve a stable defensive superstructure which permits them to function adequately. It is striking how competent some character neurotics may be; some are eminently successful and have achieved positions of power, leadership and prominence. In some instances, it is frightening to learn how much psychopathology is covered up by successful achievement in a personage who has assumed responsibilities that involve our survival as a civilization.

I can best illustrate the clinical features of these patients and the problems they present in treatment by presenting a fairly detailed account of the analytic interaction with this type of patient.

CLINICAL MATERIAL

A middle-aged housewife seemed to be nothing but a bundle of frustrations. Her husband constantly mistreated her, her children made unreasonable demands, and her friends were selfish and inconsiderate. She lacked, however, the fixity and grimness one sees in the paranoid patient. At first, her reasons for seeking therapy when she did were unclear, but, later, it became apparent that her family and friends were seeking attachments elsewhere. The patient was feeling increasingly alienated.

Her childhood was chaotic and traumatic. Both parents beat her frequently and demanded that she shoulder the responsibility of raising her younger siblings. Her father was described as an unpredictable alcoholic. She never knew what to expect from him—a caress or a blow. She believed that her mother was more consistent for varying periods of time, although from the patient's description it seemed that her mother was suffering from periodic agitated depressions. She recalled episodes lasting months on end when her mother was warm and loving and felt very much concerned about her daughter's welfare. Paradoxically, the patient felt uncomfortable and anxious at these times. After such benevolent periods, she would find herself in physical jeopardy, since the mother had violent outbursts and continuously attacked her in the midst of much agitation and tears.

I rather quickly formed the impression that, in spite of all this, she was not seriously uncomfortable, at least in the present. It seemed that she wanted me to fight with her, but I did not see this as being typically sadomasochistic, although at times there was considerable masochism. I concluded that she wanted to preserve the atmosphere of the battlefield rather than experience or inflict pain.

She was critical of just about everything and would spend hours telling me how I should decorate my office, dress, and, in general, conduct my life. One could easily become annoyed with her in terms of the content of this material. After several months of this behavior, I interpreted that she had a need to see me as an opponent since I continued doing things the way I liked instead of catering to her ideas and preferences. I emphasized that she was more interested in the battleground than the actual issues, since what she was harping upon were minor points and matters of personal taste that usually are not disputed. She quickly replied, calmly to my surprise, that high-ranking military strategists always fascinated her and she had often fantasied herself standing over a huge map, planning campaigns, while at the same time she could visualize the enemy playing the same game. She rather animatedly told me of a rather complicated game she recently bought, one in which armies are at war with each other; this game delighted her.

The next day she had lost all her exuberance. She had an air of wistful melancholy which she could not associate to anything in particular. She then reported her first dream.

An amorphous person (she could not distinguish whether male or female) came to her with a club, but she was not frightened. She knew that she would not be hit and enjoyed the challenge of being what she later called the "artful dodger."

She pictured me as the amorphous attacker. Since I sat behind her she did not have a clear picture of me. She said all of this spontaneously, and then added that she felt sad as she thought further about the dream. She was beginning to believe that I was not at all like the person with the club, and this upset her. She now thought of me as a warm, generous person who wanted to understand her, and this made her feel miserable.

Primitive pregenital elements now emerged, rather than associations expressing the more obvious sexual implications of the dream. Instead of playfully enjoying herself as she seemed to be doing in the dream, she presented herself as anxious and desperate. True, she was begging for a fight, but, at the same time, she saw herself as falling apart. This dream was followed by many dreams of houses crumbling and of drowning, but unlike the usual dream of this type which signifies structural collapse, all of these catastrophes occurred in a pleasant setting. She then had the following dream.

She was dressed in tattered rags and walking in a dirty slum. As she continued walking, this disordered ghetto gradually changed into a well-lit, spacious, clean, rich neighborhood. She then found herself facing a beautiful, large mansion, but at this precise moment she "disappeared." She felt tremendous anxiety and awakened.

The dream was difficult to describe, since she felt panic and thought of herself as a flimsy and empty shadow. After reporting this nightmare, she had an angry outburst at me, stressing the unmanageable frustration she was suffering.

I commented that, in the dream, she would have felt safer and more comfortable in the slum, and that she had made me into a mansion. She quietly agreed and then pointed out that she wanted to make me into a slum, so that I would be as dirty, horrible and angry as she was, but it was my stubborn refusal to be anything but kind and understanding that made her feel so miserably frustrated. *The analytic setting was at variance with the ambience she needed to construct, one that would permit her to project infantile needs and feelings.* She elaborated on the importance of the surrounding environment. She remembered a story she had either seen in a motion picture or heard in a soap opera on the radio during childhood, a story that had left an indelible impression on her mind. A kind and beautiful heiress brings a disheveled, deprived ragamuffin into her large, luxurious home where she has provided for the child a playroom full of toys. There is also a table full of all kinds of candy and other delicacies. The heiress leaves the child alone to contemplate and enjoy her miraculous good fortune. As soon as the heiress is out of sight, the little girl quietly walks to the window and climbs out, running back to the slums as fast as she can.

The patient wanted to see me just as she saw herself; she wanted me to be "at the same level." She had to externalize her feelings and attitudes and to perceive the outside world in the same terms as she viewed her inner organization. She could not integrate her experience with me with her usual perception of the world. She reported that it was especially difficult to be with a person who was interested in her needs and wanted to understand her. This was both indulgent and perplexing.

During the course of treatment, she began to realize that there might be some hope of raising herself from the "slum level" to the level she attributed to me. Her view of me remained favorable, but it was primitive insofar as it had megalomanic elements. But the "mansion" was not unattainable. She had after all created it herself. If she could ascribe such qualities to me, it was possible then that they could also become part of her psyche.

The fact that the analytic relationship survived her regressive need to make it into something chaotic and degraded was also helpful. The analysis continued without any disrupting complications, though it had many difficult moments.

The patient's narcissistic balance is particularly interesting. She needed to make me part of an environment, a private reality, that was familiar to her and with which she could cope. Nevertheless, she projected omnipotent grandiosity into me. She gave me qualities that narcissistic character neuroses use as defenses in order to protect them from their basic feelings of inadequacy, vulnerability and helplessness. These qualities could not survive in the reality she habitually created for herself so she projected them into me. In so doing, she revealed something interesting about symbiosis and fusion states.

She felt that being different can be dangerous; I have encountered this feeling in many other patients suffering from characterological problems. She found it terrifying to fuse with someone who is different from herself, someone who is at a "different level." One could not effect such a fusion without being destroyed. The person with the greater structural organization would amalgamate, swallow up, destroy the other. The reverse would be impossible because a lesser organization could not integrate a greater organization. Thus, she had to make me the way she saw herself, and this would be congruent with her private reality.

If we were alike, a symbiotic fusion would be safe and perhaps useful. If I were the same as she, then fusing with me would only lead to an extension of her boundaries, but it would not threaten her status as a distinct person with an autonomous organization. If good qualities were to be found outside of herself, then fusion would cause them to become part of herself. The fact that the environment she had to create was a harsh, cruel one, on the surface, seems paradoxical, but she was familiar with it and this gave her security. However, she felt alienated from the world in general.

The Patient's Private Reality and the Therapeutic Setting

My patient simply could not cope with a warm and non-threatening environment. I have encountered other patients with character disorders who reacted in a similar fashion. They react to a benign situation as if it were beyond their level of comprehension. These patients do not have the adaptive techniques to interact with a reasonable environment. Their formative years were irrational and violent. Since they make this chaos and upheaval a part of themselves, their inner excitement may clash with surroundings that differ from the infantile environment. When the world becomes benign and generous, the patient may withdraw in panic just as my patient described herself doing during a phase of ego dissolution. This was particularly emphasized by the story of the heiress and the slum child.

This woman's requirements of the world are those often seen in persons who have suffered much trauma in childhood. Their egos have become acclimated to a frustrating environment. The person with a character neurosis expects and brings about his failure. He adapts himself to life by feeling beaten in a harsh, ungiving world. To the observer, this may seem as if it were an inability to adapt, but the character neurotic, in this peculiar way, achieves synthesis in what seems to be a relentless, unrewarding struggle. This situation is different from a masochistic adjustment that is designed to effect a psychodynamic balance; the defensive constellation of my patient was vital in maintaining a total ego coherence instead of dealing with discrete conflicting disruptive impulses.

My patient was attributing a particular level of integration to reality, a process better described as *externalization*. She had a need to be frustrated. This is different from simple projection of hostile wishes onto an external object who thereby becomes transformed into a persecutor. Rather, her need to be frustrated represents a mode of adjustment that made the interaction between the ego and the reality possible. According to Freud (1911), the patient projects destructive inner impulses. This patient projected a frustrating environment. Externalization provided her with a setting where she could use adjustive and defensive techniques she had acquired during her early development. Although there is always some projection in every externalization (insofar as the construction will invariably involve the attributing of unacceptable impulses to external objects), there are additional factors.

Externalization can be conceptualized as the placing of *ego mechanisms* into the outer world, whereas the defense mechanism commonly called projection deals with impulses, affects and aspects of self and object representations that are closer to the id than to reality. For example, if the ego's chief adjustive modality is repression, then the psyche seeks a repressive environment, But, if the ego makes its adaptation to a world perceived as full of rage and violence, then acting out may be the chief interaction with the environment. The acting out displayed by my patient, however, was not flagrant antisocial behavior. She externalized her feelings by trans-forming them into actions, that is by relating in an active manner to some segment of the external world. Thus, the ego seeks its adjustment, not in a vacuum, but in a reality that supports its defenses and this may be a painful and frustrating reality.

Brody (1965) describes externalization as "distancing . . . without separation." According to him, projection also occurs, but the manipulation of reality referred to as externalization has the "purpose of verifying the projection." Other aspects of reality are simply not perceived.

OTHER DEFENSIVE ADAPTATIONS AND TECHNICAL DIFFICULTIES

I have just described a mode of adjustment, externalization, which may manifest itself by frustration, struggle and repeated failures. Patients with character neuroses display other adap-tive characteristics which, from the viewpoint of others, seem to be eminently successful, or unrewarding and futile. Successful adjustment is sometimes seen in those character neuroses which are often referred to as narcissistic characters. I wish to make some remarks about the adaptations and de-fenses which characterize this group.

These patients are frequently able to deal effectively with reality. Often they are highly successful, hardworking and very skillful at favorably impressing their associates. They seem to make their way through life easily and smoothly.

These narcissistic characters are increasingly coming to the attention of analysts. The fact that they seek analytic help belies the picture of invulnerability and self-containment that they lavishly present and which may either charm or infuriate the onlooker. Underneath a strong and arrogant exterior, the analyst is frequently confronted with a frightened, confused, helpless infantile orientation.

I am emphasizing that, in spite of wide differences in the surface picture, these narcissistic patients, from a structural viewpoint, are not significantly different from those patients just described who use externalization as a prominent adaptive modality and who seem to be alienated and vulnerable rather than confident and successful.

Their defenses and adjustments are primarily overcompensatory and they ruthlessly find their way in a world that values success. To the degree that they create a world in which they can find material rewards, attention and praise, they are also externalizing some parts of their psyche. They hold themselves together on the basis of having megalomanic expectations fulfilled. They then create a world in which they can gratify their omnipotent needs. If they succeed, then one has a picture of narcissistic fulfillment—a well-functioning integrated organism with a minimum of human qualities and feelings.

This type of character neurosis is commonly seen—a plastic, hardworking and perhaps unscrupulous person who achieves, usually for his self-enhancement and power, but sometimes with significant effect on the world. In creating a world that supports his narcissistic balance, he may actually change the world we live in. The previous examples of externalization I have given related to an already existing segment of the world. The patients did not really create it; they found something that was already there. At the most, they may have made manifest certain latent tendencies in the environment. The narcissistic patient usually does much more than that and in many instances has a tremendous effect on society for better or worse, although basically he is not concerned with maintaining a certain level of self-esteem in order to prevent psychic collapse. The latter means the prevention of a state of helpless vulnerability, one where he finds himself at the mercy of external forces and assault—in other words, an external world that will use him for its own needs and thereby stamp out all vestiges of individuality and autonomy. Therefore, the patient has to be constantly on top of the situation by seeking total control and invulnerability. These are narcissistic defenses that lead to mastery. As can be readily understood, this is a different view of the role of narcissism as it is involved in psychopathology than viewing it as the outcome of fixation at the developmental stage of primary or secondary narcissism.

Not all patients with narcissistic character neuroses are successful. Undoubtedly, the achievement of success is the outcome of many factors, not simply a response to a psychopathologically constructed defensive need. Talent obviously is involved and, no matter how pressing the need, if the person is not sufficiently gifted, he will not be able to obtain the narcissistic gratification he so badly needs.

Perhaps most of these patients are patients because they have failed in extracting from the external world sufficient narcissistic supplies to avoid feeling the consequences of their ego defects and vulnerabilities. One often sees pathetic attempts to appear powerful and competent; the more these patients fail, the greater their megalomania. The patient's adaptive and defensive attempts may establish a vicious circle. As he fails in his attempts at achieving magical control (magical because he does not have the ability to make the inner world congruent with the external world), his feeling of basic inadequacy and vulnerability correspondingly increases. This leads to a need for further narcissistic enhancement which once more encounters frustration. The more he is frustrated, the more inadequate he will feel and the greater the omnipotence he will need to protect him from his vulnerability. Thus, the vicious circle continues.

Many patients with character neuroses present lives punctuated with failure, and they often seek treatment with a sense of pressing urgency. From a particular viewpoint, all patients with character neuroses could be considered examples of narcissistic character neurotics. These patients, as a group, have an intense need to be protected from their basic sense of vulnerability. Some achieve psychic equilibrium by being successful in obtaining narcissistic supplies. Others, as discussed, are not successful, but this represents a failure of defensive adaptation. They will seek narcissistic supplies, but their structural defects are closer to the surface than is the case for the well compensated narcissist. Rather than the arrogant self-confidence that is commonly found in narcissistic patients, the character neurotics who fail to achieve often insist they are helpless, inadequate and needful, but, in spite of their obvious and perhaps flamboyant self-depreciation, they still have a discernible, if poorly hidden, arrogance. Although frightened and intimidated, their attitude toward the external world can be sneering and contemptuous.

As is true for so many patients suffering from ego defects, identity problems are prominent in character neurotics and their attempts to establish some cohesion to the self-representation may take several characteristic forms. I have already mentioned narcissistic overcompensation. Now, I wish to discuss several other typical constellations that are designed to achieve cohesion of the identity sense and narcissistic equilibrium. These are defensive and adjustive attempts which usually fail, much in the same manner that is seen in some patients who cannot maintain an exalted position which protects them from their vulnerability. Actually, as already mentioned, these attempts are very similar to those seeking narcissistic gratification. I am, in fact, discussing a variation of narcissism, the only difference being that omnipotence and grandiosity are not so obviously manifest.

I am referring to a commonly encountered group of patients, especially among college students and other young adults, although they are found in older age groups as well, who are always engaged in some activity or project but never finish it. In some instances, they never start it, although they are constantly talking about it and planning. The student who is always writing the dissertation that he will never finish is a typical example. I recall the incredible situation of a man who has been working on his Ph.D. degree for 30 years. He has been "finishing" his thesis all this time, and the fact that a ridiculous amount of time has passed never occurs to him. He still talks about it as if he were going to graduate next week and ignores the fact that this next week has been coming for three decades.

These patients are, as one of them said, in a state of "becoming." They have to be involved in something, an activity that the external world accepts as one that leads to the consolidation of an identity, in these cases a vocational or professional identity. As long as they have such a project to fasten themselves upon, they feel they have a mission and purpose in life. They feel they exist and this helps establish an autonomous boundary. The pathetic aspect of all this is that it finally becomes obvious to everyone, except to the patient, that a condition almost built into their project is that they will never achieve it. For example, with the patient who has been finishing his dissertation for 30 years, there is practically a delusional quality to his belief that he will complete his project in just a few days. How he can continue being sincere in such a conviction is incredible. It becomes apparent that without such a project these patients would have nothing to give meaning to their lives. The achievement of their goal would be frightening because it is beyond their integrative capacities.

Constant striving to define oneself seems to be typical of many persons suffering with character neuroses. This may take many forms other than those just described. Much of the peculiar and flamboyant behavior that has become so familiar in the present generation is the result of adaptational attempts—the outcome of a need to find oneself, to find a place in the universe where one might fit. The drug culture, homosexuality, deviant life-styles, and participation in analysis often prove to be manifestations of adjustive integrations so that the ego can feel itself as distinct and unassaulted.

One hears of so many therapeutic approaches that are aimed at strengthening the patient's relationship to reality. But whose reality? This is the therapist's reality, of course; there is no consideration of whether the way the therapist constructs the world is consonant with the patient's value system, background, orientation, and character structure in general. I often hear of a realistic, limit-setting, no-nonsense approach to these patients, one aimed at controlling acting-out. Again, these are the therapist's limits and more likely than not *acting-out is defined as behavior the therapist cannot stand*. The character neurotics, because of their need to externalize, that is, to construct an environment which replicates that of their traumatic infancy, seem to call into play our need to control. Perhaps being faced with other realities and other value systems is inherently threatening; this may be the basis for many of our countertransference difficulties.

Some of these struggles in therapy resemble, in microcosm, the generation gap seen more generally in conflicts between generations. One cannot help but wonder whether the prevalence of character neuroses means that we are confronted with a new type of psychopathology or whether we are being confronted with basically the same types of emotional problems but with different manifestations. Reichard (1956) reexamined some of Freud's classical descriptions of his patients and concluded that they were also suffering from severe structural problems. I am inclined to believe that the manifestations of psychopathology have changed but not the underlying psychopathology, and that these changes are reflections of differences between our contemporary social-cultural milieu and that of Freud. The process involved in the relationship between culture and the construction of psychopathology, processes which are bi-directional, are beyond the scope of a clinically oriented study and extend beyond the realm of psychoanalysis.

The character neuroses may be especially threatening to therapists, just as adolescents are threatening to adults. The age of the patient does not matter; it is the nature of his adaptations that upsets the analyst and sometimes society's equilibrium and causes both to react in a fashion that is aimed at gaining control of behavior. Not all of this behavior is basically antisocial in that it is criminal or destructive. Most of the time, it is antagonistic to current ideology.

As analysts, we have to face the fact that sometimes we do not want to be analysts. This may be inevitable and determined by our innate values and orientations, by the nature of our externalizations, by the world we construct for ourselves. The character neuroses cause us to reflect on basic issues about emotional problems, since they present us with conflicting realities rather than intrapsychic conflicts. If there has to be change, where does it begin?

Not all patients can or should be analyzed, which may help to explain why other therapeutic approaches are so popular. I regret that these approaches are often confused with analysis and sometimes described in such a fashion that they appear to be analytic. They are disguised as analysis, the focus ostensibly being on intrapsychic factors and transference issues.

I repeat, not all patients can or should be analyzed. Many patients with character neuroses have been successfully analyzed and, in terms of their psychopathology, they do not, as a group, present us with problems that are intrinsic contraindications to analysis. They threaten our beliefs and they challenge our most cherished principles and *modus operandi*, our striving for the achievement of maximum autonomy, as well as our methods for attaining this goal. The character neuroses test to the utmost our analytic dedication and, inasmuch as they do, we pronounce them to be difficult cases. True, they are difficult, because they force us to examine what is going on within ourselves. This is an intrinsic consequence of the unfolding of the transference and occurs in every analysis. However, it occurs to a greater extent with the character neuroses because they demand that we reexamine our values—the same explicit demand we make of all our patients. If we balk at this task, we should not be surprised that patients do the same, nor should we demand that patients do what we refuse to do. The question then is not one of analyzability in the fundamental sense; it is related to our tolerance of autonomy for ourselves and our patients, and to how much we really believe in what we profess.

REFERENCES

BRODY, W. (1965). On the dynamics of narcissism, *Psychoanalytic Study of the Child* 20:165-193. New York: International Universities Press.

FREUD, S. (1911). Psycho-analytic notes on an autobiographical account of a case of paranoia (dementia paranoides). *Standard Edition of the Complete Psychological Works of Sigmund Freud*, 12:1-80. London: Hogarth Press, 1958.

REICHARD, S. (1956). A re-examination of "Studies in Hysteria," *Psychoanalytic Quarterly*, 25:155-177.

Discussion

Dr. Searles: All of Dr. Giovacchini's papers that I have heard or read are in general very congenial to my way of thinking and expressive, in large part, of the way I like to think I conduct my own practice. Rather than spend my brief time expressing appreciative remarks about the way in which his paper reminded me illuminatingly of work I'm conducting at present or have conducted in the past, however, I will try to make a few remarks that I hope will add a bit to certain areas of the paper.

I will say that my main area of discontent with his paper concerns his description of himself as responding in a consistently kindly fashion throughout the work with this patient. He is responding, one might say, as a mansion to the patient and never as a slum. In my own work with such patients it seems to me that the strain of enduring the very intense negative transferences which they develop toward me represents one of the most difficult aspects of the work, and therefore one of those aspects most in need of being reported upon and discussed in detail at meetings such as this.

One such patient with whom I am currently working seems able to get in touch with nostalgic memories of his childhood primarily through reading about or seeing an occasional movie about concentration camps and similar environments. For example, the book and movie "One Day in the Life of Ivan Denisovich" reminded him of the bleaker aspects of his childhood which were spent under the sway of an enormously harsh, depriving and, above all, impersonal kind of discipline. For instance, he and his siblings were never allowed to open the refrigerator to get second helpings of anything and were kept always on so scanty a diet that they were chronically hungry. Furthermore, they were never spanked, and there were many other details about an enormously chilling, bleak and impersonally punitive and depriving childhood.

In one session, he was experiencing such an environment as emanating from me throughout the session, and as having emanated from me, similarly, during the several years of his work with me thus far. This transference to me reached such a degree of intensity that it made me extremely uncomfortable. At the end of the session, as he started to get up from the couch, I experienced for the first time in my work with him an urge to spank him, and a fantasy of doing so. I reported this to him at the moment, and he replied, in a stand-offish, antagonized manner, "Who do you think you are?"

I am happy to report that this incident did not disrupt our work together; but I found it highly instructive. I feel sure that my response was based in part upon a dawning awareness within him of long-dissociated wishes to be spanked, but that it was based in a very significant part, also, upon my trying to put away from me his transference image of me as being so highly impersonal, and essentially nonhuman, a parental environment. It was as though I were determined to establish in his mind and, above all, reestablish in my mind that I am a warmly human parental kind of person who, for example, would give the child a spanking rather than treat him in so distantly impersonal a manner.

An example of these negative transference images to me as being a chillingly nonhuman environment was included in my book in 1960 on the non-human environment. I was seeing a hebephrenic woman in her seclusion room, and she looked about her and said, "There's a weird doctor around here that doesn't make sense to me. He's mental—he's (looking uneasily at the walls of the room) everything." I asked "Wooden?" thinking of the wood on the walls. She nodded agreement and added, "He's everywhere." I asked, "He's all 800 guys?" in reference to her having indicated earlier in the hour that there were "800 guys" present. She agreed. I want to emphasize, here, how uncomfortable that sense of my being, in her experience of me, that weird, bleak, totally nonhuman environment made me feel.

I could give other such examples, but one of my basic impressions concerning the paper by Dr. Giovacchini is that, in the patient's childhood, she was essentially, or potentially rather, a mansion to her mother, a mansion to whom the mother could not adapt as such. It is my thought that the baby offers the parent the potential of a new beginning, a different, more beautiful level of existing, emotionally. For example, Dr. Giovacchini reports in this regard: "The patient wanted to see me just as she saw herself; she wanted me to be 'at the same level.' She had to externalize her feelings and attitudes and to perceive the outside world in the same terms as she viewed her inner organization. She could not integrate her experience with me with her usual perception of the world. She reported that it was especially difficult to be with a person who was interested in her needs and wanted to understand her. This was both indulgent and perplexing." My impression was that there was, in the patient in that regard, a great deal of her being identified with her mother.

Earlier in the paper Dr. Giovacchini mentions that the patient recalled "episodes lasting months on end when her mother was warm and loving and felt very much concerned about her daughter's welfare. Paradoxically, the patient felt uncomfortable and anxious at these times. After such benevolent periods she would find herself in physical jeopardy, since the mother had violent outbursts and continuously attacked her in the midst of much agitation and tears." My thought is that during those warm, loving episodes the mother was reacting to the patient as being a mansion and the paradoxical uncomfortableness the patient felt in that setting was symbiotically conveyed from the mother. I suspect that the mother could not really stand this in any thoroughly comfortable way and had to react against this mansion that the child was being for the mother.

My impression is that Dr. Giovacchini's occupying the position of a kindly mansion for the patient during the course of his work with her rested partly upon a basis of her projecting upon him her own unconscious mansion personality-aspects—personality-aspects which the mother had been unable to adequately perceive and relate to and integrate in her relationship with her daughter, and which Dr. Giovacchini was far more successful in relating himself to and integrating and helping the patient to integrate in her own personality functioning.

I want to take one more moment here in this same connection to give a bit from a paper of mine in 1973 concerning, among other topics, some aspects of autism. I suggested that, to the extent that the analyst can come comfortably and freely to immerse himself in the autistic patient as comprising his (the analyst's) world, the patient can then utilize him, the analyst, as a model for identification, as regards the acceptance of such very primitive dependency needs, and can come increasingly to exchange his erstwhile autistic world for the world comprised of and personified by the analyst. So I want to suggest, to complete this line of thought, that I am confident that, with the clinical result which we have heard was achieved here, Dr. Giovacchini must have been doing a good bit of immersing himself in the patient as being a mansion for Dr. Giovacchini.

Dr. Kernberg: Like Dr. Searles, I feel that my overall approach is within the general theoretical range that inspires Dr. Giovacchini's work. In this regard, perhaps one problem for all of you in the audience today is that you will feel somewhat disappointed with the high level of agreement among the participants regarding the overall psychoanalytic approach to borderline patients. But, for the same reason, it seems to me important to highlight the differences, even at the risk of appearing too critical of each other.

Regarding Dr. Giovacchini's presentation, particularly the areas of disagreement: First, I had some difficulties following his statements pertaining to diagnosis. Dr. Giovacchini himself said that he didn't want to use the time here to talk about differential diagnosis rather than treatment, But, perhaps, there are more important disagreements among us than one might be aware of. I believe that it is very important to arrive first at a clear diagnosis of the patient. By diagnosis I don't mean a descriptive DSM II or III diagnosis, but, rather, a combination of a descriptive and structural diagnosis. By "structural" I mean the patient's overall personality organization. Has the patient achieved integration of the tripartite system? That is, does the patient show ego identity and a high level of defensive operations and, therefore, does his syndrome reflect a high level character pathology? Or, to the contrary, does the patient present low level or severe character pathology with identity diffusion, lack of ego integration, and predominance of primitive defensive operations? Or, does the patient have a psychotic illness, with loss of reality testing and related lack of differentiation between self- and object representations, and a tendency to present fusion phenomena in the transference and establish the symbiotic transferences that Dr. Searles has described so well?

Differential diagnosis makes an enormous difference, it seems to me, in terms of indication for analysis or modified psychoanalytic psychotherapy, in terms of the needs of external structure, or in terms of psychopharmacological treatment. I think that we have a responsibility to look into the needs of each patient in terms of the broadest possible diagnostic frame. And, therefore, I am a psychoanalyst and a general psychiatrist in terms of trying to establish such a diagnosis. This is important for treatment and prognosis. Hence, when Dr. Giovacchini talks about character neurosis and narcissistic character and the alienated patient as more or less related, or overlapping, or similar, I, quite frankly, get confused.

Another question has to do with the predominant level of regression that the patient experiences. This, also, is connected to the diagnosis. I would expect that the transference regression in borderline patients, even during transference psychosis, would have very different qualities from the transference regression in intensive psychotherapy of schizophrenic patients. The true fusion phenomena and true symbiotic development really don't take place with borderline patients, unless we broaden the terms fusion and symbiosis to such an extent that they lose their specific meanings. So I am uneasy about using what Dr. Giovacchini calls symbiotic and fusion experiences in this patient who, it seemed to me, probably presented a borderline personality but not a psychotic illness. I am not sure whether this patient presented a narcissistic personality structure. It seems so, but from what Dr. Giovacchini described I can't be certain.

A third aspect which I would criticize has to do (and this probably places me in some disagreement with both Dr. Giovacchini and, in part, Dr. Searles) with comments on the relation between the transference and past experiences. At several points Dr. Giovacchini relates what is going on in the transference of this patient with what she describes had happened in her past. I find it tempting for the therapist or analyst to take this at face value; but, the more I see patients, the more I see that the relationship between the past and the present becomes more and more complex and indirect, the sicker the patient. In other words, if we have a "good neurotic" patient in analysis, the initial history indeed often tells us much about the dynamic aspects of the patient's conflicts. In contrast, with borderline and narcissistic patients, we often find out—after years of treatment—that the past history was completely different from our first impressions. So there is a difference between present structure and transference, the intrapsychic genetic history of that structure, and the actual development history of the past. In short, we have to separate development, intrapsychic genetics, and structure. How do we get from one to the other? It seems to me that only a careful analysis of transference developments gradually gives us that explanation. In the case example that Dr. Giovacchini mentioned, I had difficulties in following this. Dr. Searles expressed what seemed to me a very plausible hypothesis regarding why the patient felt bad when mother seemed so warm, explaining what really might have been going on at a deeper level. I think that it may be that that was the situation, but I think that we don't really know. We really don't know before a full analysis, in the here and now, of what the transference means.

One element that is clear is that the patient resented being treated in a warm and friendly way. That came up again and again, but from here on I don't know why she really resented it. What was really wrong—in her view—about Dr. Giovacchini's attitude of being friendly, respectful? Why couldn't she tolerate that? He interpreted this as arising from her projection onto him of the chaotic environment of her past which she couldn't tolerate. That seems to me genetic reductionism. As a therapist, I would assume that I don't know at all why she does this, that it seems to be totally absurd that someone should treat me this way, and I would make it a task for the patient to explore this with me, if necessary, for many months. I also think the issue is not simply whether she was masochistic or not, because, what does it mean to be masochistic? One can be masochistic for many reasons. And one can hate those who treat one well for many reasons. It could have been, for example, that she had to reject anything good coming from the therapist because he represented an oedipal father figure, and because of deep unconscious guilt over her sexual impulses towards such a father figure. In other words, submission to the oedipal mother was one possibility. It could also be that she felt a deeper sense of guilt over a good relation with the therapist because she felt she didn't deserve it in connection with preoedipal aspects of guilt over ambivalence toward mother. It could be that she was under the control of a sadistic, omnipotent, primitive parental introject that forbade any good relations. Or else, it could be that she felt terribly envious of the therapist: How come the therapist could be friendly and have a nice office, if she couldn't and didn't? And the more she got from him, the more it may have activated unconscious envy in her: This, by the way, would fit into a narcissistic constellation as the diagnosis in her case. It could also be that behind her rejection of the therapist was a need to denigrate, to devalue what she had, as a defense against (projected) envy. There are many of these possibilities that need to be considered in understanding masochistic behavior. My suggestion is that, before looking into the genetics, an analytic exploration in this regard must be undertaken. The transference analysis was not, from the material that I heard, carried out fully, and was prematurely taken back to the past.

Dr. Masterson: The concept of whole object relations requires that we relate to an object that is whole both good and bad. And it is in that spirit that I'm going to discuss Dr. Giovacchini's paper. I think Dr. Giovacchini's vivid and poignant case illustration demonstrates his extraordinary grasp of theory as a professional, as well as his human ability to apply it in an intuitive, empathic, meaningful way in his work with patients. Beyond that, the paper illustrates the many ways in which we share a common clinical point of view despite some differences in theory, as well as the ways in which we differ. I shall underline what we have in common before discussing how we differ.

I think the case illustration, at least from my point of view, outlines many of the clinical characteristics which are commonly found in the borderline—for example, the chaotic past history illustrating the scapegoating of the child by the parent in which the child is depersonified by the parents and must play the role that the parents have projected upon him in order to survive. Dr. Giovacchini raised the question as to what precipitated the patient into therapy. A common precipitating factor in the borderline is that something has happened to raise separation anxiety. I think this woman's family moving from her probably interrupted her fusion fantasy and exposed her to anxiety—i.e., their withdrawal frustrated her fantasies of symbiotic union with them. Her behavior in treatment is also characteristic—externalizing what is intrapsychic onto the therapist, replaying the past in the present.

When I first read the case, before reading Dr. Giovacchini's discusssion, I thought, as he later illustrated, that she had projected what I would call her bad self onto Dr. Giovacchini and was herself acting out the role of the object. By criticizing him she was doing to him what had been done to her as a child. She was replaying the past in the present in reverse and thereby relieving anger and depression and defending herself against awareness of these affects. In this endeavor, of course, the reality of the analytic situation was denied. You'll note that Dr. Giovacchini in his therapeutic approach did not interpret this to the patient. He dealt with her externalization, as I view it, by confronting her, which is a form of limit-setting; in other words, he said to the patient, "You seem to need someone to fight with." The result of this confrontation, I think, was that the externalization or the transference acting-out was interrupted and that which it was a defense against emerged in the dream and somewhat in her behavior, her rage and depression. I agree completely with his discussions of the role of externalization, as well as the techniques to deal with it.

Now let us consider the ways in which Dr. Giovacchini and I differ. In his section on other defensive adaptations and technical difficulties I must confess to experiencing a lot of difficulty in following his discussion about the character neuroses. I think he places too great an emphasis on the general rubric character neurosis, which, I feel, is too broad a category. He does not attempt to define and distinguish between different types of character neuroses or character disorders, which can lead to a good deal of confusion. Let me illustrate—he says, for example, "in spite of wide differences in the surface picture, these narcissistic patients, from a structural viewpoint, are not significantly different from those patients just described [borderline], who use externalization as a prominent adaptive modality and who seem to be alienated and vulnerable rather than confident and successful." Although I understand clearly the clinical phenomenon he is referring to—in other words the borderline patient acts out his vulnerable self by clinging and distancing while the narcissist acts out the defense against his vulnerable self by presenting the grandiose self—I would say they are similar only in the use of the same mode, externalization. However, what they externalize, the intrapsychic structure, is really quite different; the borderline has a split object relations unit containing both a rewarding and withdrawing object and self representation, while the narcissist has a fused self-object representation of the grandiose self as the omnipotent object. The borderline is defending against an abandonment and depression, the narcissist against primitive envy and rage. What I'm trying to illustrate here is how the use of these intrapsychic structural considerations brings greater clarity to the concept of character neurosis.

We have discussed a number of times our biggest difference over the concept of therapeutic limit-setting. In the last section Dr. Giovacchini raises some objections to a therapeutic technique which he perceives and describes as follows: "approaches that are aimed at strengthening the patient's relationship to reality . . . a realistic limit-setting no-nonsense approach . . . aimed at controlling acting-out." What are his objections? He asks whose reality is the patient's relationship being strengthened to: "This is the therapist's reality, of course; there is no consideration of whether the therapist constructs the world as consonant with the patient's value system, background, orientation, and character structure in general." His other objection is that the therapist defines acting-out as behavior that he does not like and cannot stand. He follows with his interpretation of why the therapist makes this error: The character neurotic needs to externalize the traumatic past, which, in therapy, calls into play in the therapist a need to control because the therapist is threatened by other or different reality or value systems than his own.

How can these objections be answered? First, what is a limit-setting intervention? Is it an effort to control behavior that the therapist can't stand? I don't think so. I think it's an effort to bring to the attention of the patient's observing ego the denied and destructive effects of the operation of his pathologic defense mechanisms—in other words, such mechanisms as avoidance, splitting, denial, projection, projective identification, clinging and acting out. Is it behavior the therapist cannot stand? No, it is behavior which is itself an obstacle to the patient's own conscious stated objectives. Is the purpose to adapt the patient to the therapist's reality? No, the purpose is rather to bring to the attention of the patient's observing ego, and therefore to the area of conscious choice, the denied and destructive effects on his everyday life in the present of his need to externalize and replay the past.

Dr. Giovacchini's approach and my approach to patients are really quite similar, so how are we to explain this apparent discrepancy? In order to get some explanation I went back and read some of Dr. Giovacchini's writings. I would like to entitle this last section of my remarks "When is a Duck a Fish?" and begin with a story. The story is of a young Jewish man who goes into a Catholic church in order to become a Catholic. So he says, "Father, would you make me into a Catholic?" The Father says all right and takes him over to a baptismal font where he makes the sign of the cross and says some words and sprinkles some holy water on the man and then says, "Now, my son, you are a Catholic." The young man then leaves the church, walks down the street, enters a restaurant nearby, sits down to have lunch and orders duck with orange sauce. Soon after the priest comes by sees the young man eating the duck. He is absolutely horrified and says, "My son, what are you doing? You are a Catholic! It's Friday and you know you can't eat meat!" And the young man replied, "Just a minute, Father, this isn't duck, it's a fish. When the waiter brought the duck I did with it just what you did with me, I sprinkled some water on it, made the sign of the cross, said a few words, and it became a fish." The relevance of the story will become apparent in a moment.

In his book, *Psychoanalysis of Character* (Chapter 22, pp. 310-314), Dr. Giovacchini says the following, "Another technical factor necessary for analysis of these patients in addition to interpretation is the defining of the analytic setting. The analyst in a subtle fashion defines the realistic limits of the patient's reactions and indicates the quality and the extent of his counterreactions. He will react to the patient's feelings as intrapsychic phenomena of interest and worthy of study. His frame of reference is observational. This facilitates analysis and understanding of the transference."

At this point in his writing, Dr. Giovacchini uses the magic of words to change the duck of confrontation into the fish of interpretation. He says that, although defining the analytic setting could be considered supportive and could promote a therapeutic alliance, this is not really so. Defining the analytic setting is not confronting or limit-setting; it is merely another variety of transference interpretation. His theory is that there are three combinations of people in the interview: the patient analyst (transference fusion), the patient as a patient, and the analyst as an analyst. Therefore, explicit references to the analytic setting refer to transference and are directed toward acknowledging and resolving the fusion. Dr. Giovacchini through the magic of words transfers a therapeutic activity which I consider limit-setting, a confrontation, into interpretation. That duck of confrontation becomes the fish of interpretation. In my judgment, defining analytic setting is setting reality limits against which the symbolic fusion of transference can be contrasted, compared and worked through. In conclusion, the difference is not in what we do, but in how we conceptualize it.

Dr. Giovacchini: To maintain consistency with an obsessive orientation I will proceed in order of the discussions. I'll begin with Dr. Searles' remarks and lead up to Dr. Masterson. I didn't want to give the impression that my demeanor throughout this whole analysis was benign and kind and that I was not the target of negative transference feelings. Negative transference occurred and was a prominent feature of the analysis, but I didn't choose to go into that because this was not meant to be a continuous case seminar or a case study. There was only one particular purpose for presenting this material and that was to illustrate what I believe to be a mechanism that is characteristic of this type of patient, the mechanism of externalization as contrasted to the mechanism of projection. Whether the patient was a mansion to her mother, I really don't know because I don't know very much about the mother. It's hard enough to know something about the patient without trying to make inferences about someone in the patient's life. I know from my own experience that whenever I've tried to conjecture about someone else I have usually been abysmally wrong, even in my concepts and images of how some person in the patient's life looked.

Dr. Kernberg and Dr. Masterson have made comments about diagnosis, something that I really didn't want to get into because I wanted to discuss psychic mechanisms. But I would agree that this field requires diagnostic clarification. I simply didn't think that was to be our purpose today, that our purpose rather was to discuss cases that most of us have some kind of familiarity with. The patient that I'm discussing is so common that I'm certain that all of you in the audience could rather quickly think of patients of your own or people that you know who illustrate similar mechanisms. I have, as a matter of fact, worked out what for me is a comfortable diagnostic scheme. It will be published (and I am now advertising) in my forthcoming book, *Psychoanalysis of Primitive Mental States*, where I divide character disorders into five subcategories. This patient would fit into one of the more advanced states. Dr. Kernberg was saying that there are differences in the degree of regression and primitivization of the psyche, and that is quite true. I would place this patient, in contrast to other cases, as having considerably more psychic structure than other types of character disorders or psychotics.

As for the value of diagnosis in general, I think this is a controversial question, too. My own style is that I don't tend to think in diagnostic terms. The patient comes to me—now I grant that the patient that comes to me has already been selected. The patient is coming explicitly for a particular purpose. If they want drugs or hospitaliation or other kinds of therapy, they go elsewhere. So this is perhaps an artifact that doesn't help us make general judgments. In any case, I think of the patient in terms of psychic mechanisms and of structure. Whatever diagnostic opinions I may have are opinions that evolve as the transference unfolds. This is similar to what Winnicott called a therapeutic diagnosis. I don't want to have too many set ideas about it because I like to be surprised once in a while and I like to be able to link my diagnostic judgments with very specific things that are happening in the transference situation.

Dr. Kernberg states that fusion is characteristic of primitive psyches. Well, of course, fusion can also be considered in terms of a hierarchy and this patient very definitely had fusion states. I didn't go into detail, but she went into very deep regressions and there were occasions when she, like some other patients, actually didn't know who she was—where her boundaries were completely, or for the most part, dissolved; at times she referred to herself with my name, having actually forgotten her own. We even had some episodes of regressions that some of you might consider psychotic but they were manageable and they were limited to the hour.

Now as far as Dr. Kernberg's remarks about transference, I was a little puzzled because I felt that perhaps he was creating a straw man. I do not believe that genetic reconstructions as such are particularly useful for these patients and I have repeatedly stated this for many years. The patient may, on occasion, make a genetic reconstruction but the important element is, as Kernberg put it, what is occurring in the here and now, what is currently being experienced. If one wants to link it back to some figure in past life, this is often evasion on our part. The therapist may be defending himself against the transference. Relating the patient's feeling to someone in the remote past relieves the therapist from having to bear the brunt of them currently. So I really don't understand Kernberg's point or why he brought it up.

The fact that the patient felt uncomfortable in the benign environment, the question that Dr. Kernberg raised, also puzzled me. This puzzles me because that was the point of the whole paper, which is an attempt to explain externalization, to demonstrate that the patient did not have the integrative capacity, the adjustive mechanisms, to relate to a benign environment. I can give some rather startling examples that are familiar to most clinicians. The example that immediately comes to mind is that of the battle scarred master sergeant who is really quite adept and has all the adaptive techniques, all the skills, all the requirements necessary to survive in horrible battle conditions. He's comfortable with the cannons booming and the bombs exploding, whereas most of us would be frightened to death. He can adapt to that kind of environment; we can't. It's not our environment; it's not our reality but it's his reality. Still, if you take this master sergeant and put him in a nice peaceful environment he'll fall apart. I've seen examples of this not too uncommon situation when I was in the army. It's this type of process that I'm trying to illustrate in this particular patient. She is more subtle in her construction of the environment than the sergeant.

This brings me to Dr. Masterson's comments. I didn't say anything to the audience about no-nonsense limit-setting and reality, but it's in the paper; Masterson is quite right. He told me he was going to bring up this point so I left it out; I told him I was going to tone it down. Not that I don't like controversy, but I didn't particularly want to get involved with this issue, but I suppose I have to. If you wish to call my pointing out externalization a confrontation, that is acceptable. I'm not going to argue that particular point because we are not involved in a seminar today as to what constitutes an interpretation. In the paper that he quoted (which scared me a little because I don't always remember what I've written, but he picked out some pretty good passages), I went into extensive details outlining what I consider to be a transference interpretation. Pointing out the limits of my reactions within the consultation room to me was equivalent to a transference interpretation. It took me about seven pages to work that out and I was inspired to do so by an experience of Winnicott's.

Winnicott writes about a patient who became quite excited about some success he had achieved and he felt that this should affect Winnicott, too, because this achievement was the outcome of a successful analysis. Winnicott apparently did not respond properly because the patient said, "You're not getting as excited; you don't seem to be as happy about this as I am," whereupon Winnicott said, "That's true. I'm not as excited as you are, I don't feel as elated as you do, but then again I don't feel as much despair as you do either." He is pointing out that his range, his spectrum, was narrower than the patient's, and, inasmuch as the patient's range goes beyond Winnicott's, it represents projection, because he believes that Winnicott should feel the same as he does. The patient is attributing his own feelings, feelings based upon infantile expectations, onto the therapist, and this is transference. Winnicott's response would be a transference interpretation. This theme could be expanded considerably. Calling this definition of the setting confrontation seems to miss the subtle projective process that is involved. As Masterson was talking I wrote, "According to Masterson, limit-setting equals interpretation," and then he went ahead and said it and told a story about a duck and a fish.

To me, limit-setting means disapproval, a word Masterson did not use. My patient had had two other analysts before she came to me; practically all of my patients have had between two and four other analysts. Not that there was anything wrong with these analysts; they simply rejected the patients. They were setting limits, they were distpproving of behavior, they were disapproving of the manifestations of symptoms. If one can relate to the patient in terms of his reactions and behavior in a nonjudgmental fashion and leave out the note of disapproval, then I do not think it matters whether we think of confrontation or interpretation.

REFERENCES

Giovacchini, P. L. (1975). *Psychoanalysis of Character Disorders*. New York: Jason Aronson.

Giovacchini, P. L. (1978). *Psychoanalysis of Primitive Mental States*. New York: Jason Aronson.

Searles, H. F. (1960). *The Nonhuman Environment in Normal Development and in Schizophrenia*. New York: International Universities Press.

Searles, H. F. (1973). Concerning therapeutic symbiosis. *Annual of Psychoanalysis*, 1:247-262. See p. 259.

Winnicott, D. W. (1972). Fragment of an analysis, in *Tactics and Techniques in Psychoanalytic Therapy*, 455-694, ed. by P. Giovacchini. New York: Jason Aronson.

Chapter 2

Psychoanalytic Therapy

with the Borderline Adult:

Some Principles

Concerning Technique

Harold F. Searles, M.D.

Early in the development of psychoanalytic theory and technique, traumatic events in the patient's early years were regarded as having a central role in the etiology of emotional illness. In recent decades, as we have learned more about the psychodynamics of family life, nonverbal communication, and the causation and treatment of psychotic and borderline states which have their origin largely in the preverbal, or very early verbal, eras of infancy and childhood, we attach generally less significance to isolated traumatic events in the patient's developmental years. Rather, we focus attention on ongoing attitudes on the parts of various childhood-family-members toward the patient (and on his part toward them), and upon the prevailing emotional atmosphere, day after day, which pervaded the early home.

In pace with this shift in focus, it seems to me, the emphasis in our psychoanalytic technique has shifted such that interpretations are now accorded about the same order of importance, in the armamentarium which we employ during the overall course of a psychoanalytic treatment, as traumatic events are now allotted in our understanding of the causation of the patient's illness. Interpretations are important, to be sure; but of far greater importance is the emotional atmosphere or climate of the sessions, day after day and year after year.

As regards the treatment of the borderline patient, any discussion of interpretations has to be linked with the patient's predominant level of ego functioning, which, in turn, is largely a factor of the evolution and eventual resolution of the patient's transference-borderline-psychosis. Since appreciable regression can, and at times necessarily does, occur on the part of analyst as well as patient, the analyst's varying levels of ego functioning are also a highly significant variable.

My discussion here is integrally related with that which I presented in three earlier papers (Searles, 1970, 1971, 1973) concerning autism, symbiosis, and individuation. Those three modes of ego functioning I described as being of importance not only in patients suffering from schizophrenia of whatever degree of severity, but also in predominantly neurotic individuals in whom subtly present areas of autism come to light in their analyses.

In work with the borderline patient, the analyst finds that his countertransference burden consists, perhaps year after year, largely in his lack of freedom to make effective transference interpretations, in marked contrast to a later, ambivalently symbiotic, phase in the patient-analyst relationship, during which he can make such interpretations with a far higher degree of freedom and effectiveness.

In one (1970) of those three papers, entitled "Autism and the Phase of Transition to Therapeutic Symbiosis," I described as characteristic of that phase of transition that "the analyst now begins to find it feasible effectively to make transference interpretations. . . . This transition phase likewise stands in contrast, as regards the timeliness of transference interpretations, to the subsequent phase of therapeutic symbiosis, in which such interpretations are almost limitlessly in order."

This paper is confined largely to a discussion of the problems presented by the borderline patient whose ego functioning is predominantly autistic in nature. The state of his ego integration and differentiation is incomplete in characteristic ways which impair greatly his ability to utilize verbal interpretations. He is unable to differentiate, at an unconscious level, between fantasy and reality, or between verbalization and physical activity (with the result that verbal aggression, from the analyst, may have fully the impact of physical aggression). He has not yet established a durable internalized image of himself, or of his analyst, or both. He cannot function reliably in terms of both he himself and the analyst having—each of them—his own individuality and subjective reality, and with a sense of relatedness between those two persons and their respective realities. Instead, for him, either his is the only reality there is, or the analyst's reality is the only one.

One of the major technical difficulties in working with him has to do with his flawed sense of reality—not only outer but also inner reality, including that of his own identity—and his consequent need for the analyst to help him to resolve this flaw in his experience of reality. A major aspect of this difficulty, for the analyst, is his finding himself under great pressure to impose his own reality upon the patient, rather than struggling through, mutually with him, to help him to achieve a sense of reality valid for the individual patient himself. Helene Deutsch (1942), in her classic paper concerning the "as-if" type of emotionality and spurious reality-relatedness so prevalent among borderline patients, helped to alert us to the danger that such a patient will emerge from analysis with only his usual shallowly adaptive sense of reality, patterned now upon the personality functioning of the analyst, just as it had been patterned upon that of a series of parent figures prior to the analysis.

The studies concerning infantile psychosis by Mahler (1968) and her co-workers are of central importance here. She reports that

> It is the specific unconscious need of the mother that activates, out of the infant's infinite potentialities, those in particular that create for each mother "the child" who reflects her own *unique* and individual needs.
> . . .
> Mutual cuing during the symbiotic phase creates that indelibly imprinted configuration—that complex pattern —that becomes *the leitmotif for "the infant's becoming the child of his particular mother"* (Lichtenstein, 1961). . . . *What we seem to see here is the birth of the child as an individual* (cf. Lichtenstein, 1964).

Lichtenstein (1961) states that

> While the mother satisfies the infant's needs, in fact creates certain specific needs, which she delights in satisfying, the infant is transformed into an organ or an instrument for the satisfaction of the mother's unconscious needs. . . . *Out of the infinite potentialities within the human infant, the specific stimulus combination emanating from the individual mother "releases" one, and only one, concrete way of being this organ, this instru-*

ment. This "released" identity will be irreversible, and thus it will compel the child to find ways and means to realize this specific identity which the mother has imprinted upon it (pp. 18-19).

A number of authors have described their finding that the early, poorly integrated life experiences of borderline and schizoid (as well as schizophrenic) individuals can become integrated in awareness, and thus contribute to a firmer sense of reality and of personal identity, through the medium of the unfolding transference and the interpretation of that transference. Khan's (1974) writings portray, in a particularly beautiful way, the process wherein those previously unintegrated, dissociated affective experiences from the patient's early childhood are first experienced by the analyst, in the course of the psychoanalytic therapy.

The repetition compulsion is, in my view, an unconscious attempt not merely to "relive" an earlier experience, but to *live* it for the *first* time—to live it, that is, with full emotional participation.

The potential power which such a patient's transference gives to the analyst, power which when wrongly used can impose still another pseudo-reality and pseudo-identity upon the patient, is clearly enormous. In a paper entitled, "The Function of the Patient's Realistic Perceptions of the Analyst in Delusional Transference" (1972), I reported a relevant finding from my work, then more than 18 years in duration, with a chronically schizophrenic woman who long had manifested an appallingly severe ego fragmentation and identity confusion. That is, I reported my gradually discovering to what a significant degree her delusional transference experiences were reactions to (and often identifications with) various attributes, heretofore largely unconscious to me, of my own personality functioning during our sessions.

I cannot believe that any analyst can help a patient to make contact with, and to integrate, the latter's heretofore dissociated, early life experiences without some contamination by the analyst's own dissociated early life experiences, which the analyst succeeds (so to speak) in projecting upon, and leaving projected upon, the patient's childhood-self. But surely we should strive to keep such contaminants to a minimum.

Concerning more localized, but still massive, instances of the unconscious defense mechanism of denial, for something like two decades now I have felt convinced that this defense is so formidable because it is maintained with the power which is, in essence, the individual's striving for autonomy. Spitz' (1957) volume, *No and Yes—On the Genesis of Human Communication*, provided substantiation for this impression, which I had gained from work with adult patients. Spitz reported, for example, from his observations of the nursing infant, that

> The refusal [to nurse] through head-rotating avoidance emerges at the stage at which the earliest ego organization has just come into being. This form of volitional refusal behavior in the feeding situation continues during the progressive unfolding of the ego in the months which follow . . . (p. 94).

The practical relevancy of this, in my work with borderline patients whose defenses include massive denial, is that when I encounter a particularly striking instance of the patient's omission of any mention of a highly significant recent event, or of what I know to be a centrally important aspect of his current life situation, I am cautious about pointing out to him this striking omission. The reason is that he is too quick to foster his intendedly free-associational role's becoming, instead, the familiar one of his being the object of intended brain-programming by the analyst. That is, it often feels impossible for me to point out to him that he has said nothing about such-and-such a subject without my conveying at the same time the implication that he has not been free associating "correctly"—that he should have been reporting thoughts and feelings about that particular subject instead.

This state of patient-analyst interaction should, theoretically, be susceptible of interpretation to the patient—including interpretation of his largely unconscious wishes to be brainwashed rather than to become a full-fledged partner with the analyst in their mutual endeavor, an endeavor which involves both their brains and their two individual selves. Equally important would be any interpretations of the patient's projection upon the analyst, here, of the patient's own unconscious aim of brain washing the analyst in a single-mindedly authoritarian fashion. Stierlin's (1959) paper, "The Adaptation to the 'Stronger' Person's Reality—Some Aspects of the Symbiotic Relationship of the Schizophrenic," is relevant to this subject.

But in actual practice, I rarely, if ever, find that these highly resistant patients are accessible to such interpretations. As a result, I come, more and more as the years go on, to leave it to them largely to arrive at their own interpreting of their conflicts and their characterologic defenses against those conflicts. I have come to count it as a rare instance of job-satisfaction when I find a patient coming, bit by bit, to discover, on his own and largely unhindered by me, some important aspect of his ego functioning which has been obvious to me, and has seemed to me tantalizingly close to being interpretable by me, for many months and, in many instances, for several years.

Parenthetically, but in a similar vein, I have come a long way from my beginning-analyst's burdened sense of conviction that if a patient has succeeded in remembering a detailed dream and, beyond that, in reporting relatively voluminous associations to the dream, it is unthinkable for me to fail to offer an interpretation. A very considerable share of my time, since those early days in my analytic career, has been spent in working with borderline patients whose voluminous reports of dreams, as well as free-associational reporting, clearly have been in the service of their unconsciously giving me to feel the sense of uselessness and uncreativeness and deadness which has been one of their own most centrally important dissociated ego aspects. I have come to believe, moreover, that this more fundamental state of things in the transference will not be interpretable, as such, for probably many months or even some years, and I have learned that the sooner I can come to accept this degree of resistance on the patient's part, rather than continuing to pound against it with interpretations—no matter how perceptive and sagacious, the sooner will come the glad day of his becoming more collaboratively related with me. Here the concept of therapeutic symbiosis, which I have discussed in several earlier papers (1959, 1965, 1970, 1971, 1973, 1976) is pertinent.

In my work with the borderline patient, I find that he can come to accept my help in his achieving a sense of reality valid for him only after, and to the degree that, I have first proved able to accept the reality of his transference to me. In oversimplified terms, he can let me define reality for him only after he has thus defined my reality. I hasten to explain to you, here, that I do not mean that the analyst must have come to accept the "reality" imposed upon him by the patient's transference image(s) of him as being the analyst's *only* reality; were that to develop, the analyst clearly would have become a partner in a *folie à deux*. What I do mean is that the analyst, before he can help the patient to achieve a valid and durable sense of reality (one which is consonant, although far from identical, with the analyst's own sense of reality), must first have come to sense the impact of the patient's transference images of him. This impact has a full reality-value for the patient, and is sufficient to give rise in the analyst to a set of feeling-experiences which become identifiable, over the course of the months and years, as a *kind* of coherent countertransference-psychosis or countertransference-borderline-psychosis. Although this is of intendedly manageable proportions, it is, nonetheless, a relatively distinct affect-laden structure in the countertransference.

Once the analyst has become able to experience this impact of the patient's transference-reality, and has become accustomed enough to find it tolerable, he will not need to flee in submerged panic from this imposed transference role by attempting prematurely to interpret to the patient the ego contents which the latter is projecting upon him. It has seemed to me, in working with one patient after another through such developments, that if I myself am finding the particular transference role in question to be so intolerably upsetting to me, how can I as yet expect the patient, whose ego-organization is much less strong than my own, to be able to integrate these so-anxiety-laden dissociated ego-components which he is projecting upon me?

Now I shall comment briefly upon the importance, in particularly difficult cases, of utilizing, in one's interpretations, the patient's own phraseology and emotional tone. Marie Coleman Nelson and her co-workers' (1968) techniques of what they call paradigmatic psychotherapy (a paradigm being defined as a showing or saying by example), for treating borderline and other patients who are inordinately resistive to the usual techniques of verbal interpretation, are of interest here. While I do not embrace paradigmatic techniques in my own psychoanalytic work, primarily for the reason that these involve, for my taste, too much of a deliberate attempt to influence what should be a more spontaneously evolving transference-and-countertransference process, I find the detailed studies by Nelson and her colleagues to merit careful study.

Something like 25 years ago, Clarence G. Schulz, then a colleague of mine on the Chestnut Lodge staff, emphasized the importance, in work with schizophrenic patients, of giving interpretations which are oriented toward the patient's view of things, rather than one's own. This immediately struck me as sound, and has been very much part of my technique, in working with patients generally, since then.

Similarly, long ago, I started learning the importance of using, whenever feasible, the patient's own vocabulary in making interpretations, for I have been through many painful experiences of finding that words from my own customary vocabulary which I had assumed to be entirely acceptable synonyms for various of the patient's words proved to have an entirely different, and often very upsetting, meaning to him. One of my most frequent modes of interpreting is to acknowledge the patient's conscious view, using his own phraseology, but then adding a bit of elaboration to this, which is intendedly interpretive in effect.

During the past seven years or so, I have learned, similarly, that some of the most difficult patients can hear interpretations only if these are delivered in the affective tone characteristic of the patient's own mode of speaking. This finding is consonant with an impression I have long had, that in early ego development the first experienced separate object tends to be sensed as a twin of oneself. That is, in work with a highly autistic patient, one may find that he can register one in his awareness sufficiently to attend to a brief interpretation only if this is sensed as coming from, essentially, a twin of the patient himself.

For example, in my work with one extremely rigid woman, I seldom found, over the years, occasion for making an interpretation, and found that more than nine-tenths of those I made, over all the years, proved ineffectual so far as I could determine. This woman customarily reported, throughout each session, in a tone (irrespective of the content) of upbraiding me, lecturing me in a domineering fashion, and chronically, in a tone of barely suppressed—nearly uncontrollable—fury. After several years of work with her, I began finding that on those occasions when I made an interpretation which proved effective, I had made it in a tone of barely controlled fury—a tone practically identical with one of her own customary tones.

In my work with this woman, it eventually became clear that, to her, I was alive only when I was speaking in such a tone. In my work with her and with other patients similar in this regard but with illnesses of various diagnoses, I have found the phrase "controlled tirade" to be accurately descriptive both of the patient's daily tone during analytic sessions, and of the needed tone on the analyst's part in conveying interpretations.

More speculatively, I surmise that at different phases of an analysis interpretations need to be made in various forms and affective tones. For example, when the patient is in a phase of exploring predominantly oral conflicts, interpretations may need to be made in a spirit of feeding; when he is in a predominantly anal phase, in a spirit facilitative of increasingly well-controlled catharsis; when he is in a phase of exploring genital-sexual conflicts, in a spirit of well-sublimated sexual interaction with him. I know this all sounds thoroughly contrived; but what I am attempting to suggest, here, is that the analyst's mode of participating *inevitably will* vary, from one phase of the analysis to another, under the influence of the patient's varying transference reactions to him. And I am trying to suggest that the more aware we can become of such variations in our own mode of participation, the more capably we can exercise these in a basically non-contrived manner. Surely the level of the patient's ego-development, at any particular phase of the analysis, will be relevant for the length or brevity of our interpretations, and I believe the affective tones, however subtle, will naturally vary also.

It can be said more confidently, here, that in any case the analyst will be well advised to be attentive to the nature of the patient's varying transference reactions to his interpretations, throughout different phases of the analysis. Is he unconsciously reacting to one's having given him an interpretation as being equivalent to one's having been giving him to suck at the breast, or as being the equivalent of anal intercourse, or as being a matter of one's holding him in the refuge of one's maternal arms, or as being a disavowal of the emotional oneness which had prevailed just before one launched into the interpretation, or what?

Patients' transference reactions to the analyst's *silences* are, I believe, a relatively neglected area in the literature, and an important one in the work with borderline patients, whose transference-reactions and -attitudes are oftentimes so strikingly distorted. It has been no great surprise to me to discover that a patient has been reacting, for months or years, to my being silent as equivalent to my being dead, or my being psychotically immersed in my own fantasy world, or my being senile, or my being an inanimate object of some sort. But it has been startling to me to find that one borderline patient unconsciously experienced my being silent throughout nearly all of each session as being a matter of my incessantly lecturing him in a primly critical and self-righteously condemnatory fashion. A borderline woman expressed grating rage and fury concerning a male supervisor whom she found to be outspokenly and verbally critical of her, on frequent occasions. Several minutes later, after I had continued to be silent, she said, "I guess in your silence I see you as being that kind of disparaging, mocking, sneering person."

In the work with a borderline man who digresses endlessly, branching off repeatedly from his own intended main path in reporting his associations, I have been astonished to find that he reacts to my sitting there, silently, as being a matter of my repeatedly interrupting him. It became evident that he felt I should be controlling so closely what he was saying that, when I silently allowed him to digress, I was in effect fully and forcefully and verbally interrupting him, maddeningly, from pursuing his intended main theme. The fact that he was feeling interrupted by me was not promptly and explicitly declared by him; it had first to be inferred from relatively subtle evidence in his behavior, posture, and vocal tones. As regards what is going on in the patient at such a juncture, I think of this as a phenomenon of one of the introjects coming in and interrupting the presently-being-manifested introject, and it requires only a minute sign of the analyst's presence for the interrupting introject to be projected upon the analyst. But I have found such patient reactions to occur, toward me, even at times when I was not only silent but motionless, and have found many times that only a slight variation in the sound of my breathing is sufficient to evoke the patient's feeling maddeningly interrupted by me.

I surmise that in working with any patient of whatever diagnostic category, my silence is my most reliably effective therapeutic tool; surely this is the case in my work with borderline individuals. One patient after another eventually comes in the course of therapy to realize that, as one put it with surprise, "Your silence must really be getting to me," whereas all, or nearly all, verbal interpretations have failed to do so.

It is easy for an analyst to maintain an unexamined illusion that so long as he is being silent he is functioning, essentially, in an emotionally neutral fashion during the session, in the best classically analytic tradition. It is well for us to realize, on the contrary, that patients' diverse transference reactions to one's silence have, in all probability, some significant basis in the reality of the *kind* of silence one is presenting to them. Just as we find patients' silent demeanors to cover a wide range of feeling-states—from emotional remoteness to hopelessness to discouragement to sexually seductive invitingness to paranoid stonewall antagonism to whatever—so we need to be attentive to the fact that the particular *kind* of silence we are manifesting, at any one moment, may be anything but dispassionate. It has been difficult but helpful for me to realize, for instance, in my work with one or another borderline patient who was much given to paranoid-antagonistic silences, that my own silence was in all probability being experienced by him, to a degree quite accurately, as being of essentially that same inhospitably stonewall, or bristlingly antagonistic, threatened and threatening nature. As I have come to see these things more clearly, it has been less baffling to me to find that the patient is having great difficulty in associating at all freely and in reporting to me such associations.

On the more positive side, regarding what "kind" of silence the analyst is manifesting—that is, what is the specific nature of his nonverbal relatedness with the patient—I have come to believe that, when I have discovered in the patient some largely unconscious conflict concerning which I remain, then, for many months or even some years silent, knowing it would be premature, yet, to give the patient an interpretation concerning this conflictual area, my *nonverbal* responsiveness to or participation with him is changed, nonetheless, very significantly as a result of my discovery. For example, if I discover that the patient has an unconscious conflict from negative-oedipal sources concerning me as a parent-figure of the same sex as himself (or herself), I do not doubt that this discovery causes me to behave, in however minute and subtle

ways, differently thereafter toward him or her, until his conflict comes sufficiently fully into his awareness to be subject
to interpretation and resolution. Whether I behave, meanwhile, in a bit more seductive, or a bit more stand-offish, way
—or, more likely, a combination of both, from one time to
another—I cannot say. However, I am convinced that after
the analyst has made such a discovery, even though the patient may hear no interpretation from him concerning this
for, say, many months, he has reason to sense, at no matter
how unconscious or preconscious a level, that the analyst is
responding differently to him. Further, I surmise that this
subtly changed nonverbal participation on the part of the
analyst helps to enable the patient to become aware of the
feelings and memories in question, and to be able to listen to
and integrate verbal interpretations concerning this previously unconscious material.

What I am endeavoring to do here is to describe, more adequately than one generally finds it described in the literature,
what is really transpiring between analyst and patient while
the analyst is being silent. It is of fundamental importance for
us to become as free as possible from any illusions concerning
silence on the analyst's part as being automatically equatable
with neutral, even-hovering attention. Surely 90% of most
analysts' time with most patients is spent with the analyst's
being silent, and in the work with many a borderline patient,
98 to 99% of one's time involves one's being nonverbal with
him.

The videotaping of psychoanalytic sessions, despite all the
difficulties so gross a parameter would introduce into the
analysis, would help to bring what I am suggesting here
down from the realm of speculation and into clinically docu-

mented and established form. We need, in this regard, studies of adult psychoanalysis which are comparable, in minuteness of detailed observation, to those of Spitz (1957), of Mahler and her co-workers (1968, 1975) and others concerning the mutual cuing which occurs between a mother and her infant. Berger (1970) is one of those who are pioneering in video-tape techniques which hold considerable promise for such psychoanalytic research in the future.

Next, I want to make two points concerning the interpretation of the patient's identifications. First I wish to emphasize the suicidal-despair-engendering effect of one's interpreting, too early, that much of what the patient has felt to be the core of his self consists, instead, in large part, in an unconscious identification (introject) derived from experience with a parent. Patients generally are very resistant, naturally enough, to discovering that *precisely* that which they have most assumed to be their very own self is, to a high degree, comprised of such an introject. A premature interpretation of such an introject or unconscious identification is especially injurious if the analyst gives the interpretation in a spirit of disavowing implicitly that he himself possesses, in his own personality functioning, any appreciable element of the particular personality traits in question. An interpretation so given tends to foster the patient's feeling isolated from (a) his usual sense of identity, (b) his parent from whom the introject had been largely derived, and (c) the analyst. Particularly if the analyst is implicitly disavowing of his own part in all this, the patient is likely to be feeling burdened essentially with a projected part-aspect of the analyst's own unconscious, which the patient feels pressured, now, to acknowledge as being his own real identity. All this is comparable with the position in which the analyst so often finds himself —of feeling under intense pressure to acknowledge that the patient's intensely felt transference image of him is his, the analyst's, only real identity.

In a recent paper, I (Searles, 1978) described that the analyst can discover that his "own" feelings in working with any one patient are comprised in large part, layer under successive layer, of countertransference elements—comprised, that is, of responses and attitudes which are natural and inherent counterparts to the patient's transference responses and attitudes toward him. My second point, now, is an analogous one: namely, that any one area of a patient's identification with a parent has, beneath its relatively superficial layer, successive layers of deeper lying components, or ramifications, of this identification.

For example, in a recent dream a patient found herself living the life of a hermit in a desolate house, the bleakness of which was relieved only superficially by an attractively colorful wall-covering in one of the rooms. The wall-covering was of the same color, she commented, "as this wall-covering' '(i.e., in my office). Other associations, from this and other sessions, indicated that behind her superficial cheerfulness, which involved much identification with her mother and which had some counterpart in my own demeanor at times, was a realm of depressive bleakness which involved, in turn, identification with affective impoverishment in her mother and which had a counterpart, again, in some of the components of my own personality. That is, the dream was saying something not merely about colorfulness on the analyst's (= mother's) part, but also about underlying loneliness and bleakness.

A patient who suddenly takes a week's vacation, shortly after the analyst has taken one, can readily be seen to be doing so on a basis, in part, of a kind of spiteful identification with the analyst. But the particular ways in which the patient does this need to be evaluated in terms of whether these also represent less conscious identifications with the analyst in terms of the patient's transference perceptions of him. For example, it may well develop that the patient's sudden and spiteful announcement of his own forthcoming vacation betrays unconscious identifications with the analyst who is perceived, unconsciously, by the patient as having given too little notice of a vacation which the analyst was bent on taking, and was taking predominantly as a means of spiting the analysand.

Further, as I have learned in relatively recent years, any acting-out in which a patient becomes involved during his vacation is very likely to be based to a significant degree upon identifications with his analyst's vacation activities, according to the patient's unconscious fantasies concerning the analyst—no matter how farfetched these initially may seem, in terms of the analyst's and analysand's conscious images of the former's extra-analytic living.

In closing, I want most to emphasize that an inner refusal, on the analyst's part, to perceive any reality basis in himself for the patient's projection-laden, transference-linked images of him inevitably boomerangs in rendering him proportionately ineffective in his analytic work with the patient. Particularly in work with borderline patients (or those even more deeply ill), who tend so powerfully to become bearers of the burden of the analyst's projection of his own unconscious self-images as being, say, essentially non-human, or unfit to live, or incapable of caring, or incurably sadistic, or whatever, it is essential that the analyst become as open as possible to acknowledging to himself that even the patient's most severe psychopathology has some counterpart, perhaps relatively small by comparison but by no means insignificant, in his own *real* personality functioning. We cannot help the borderline patient, for example, to become well if we are trying unwittingly to use him as the receptacle for our own most deeply unwanted personality components, and trying essentially to require him to bear the burden of all the severe psychopathology in the whole relationship.

Summary

Although interpretations have a significant role in the analyst's work with the borderline patient, it is a *relatively* minor one by contrast to that of the analyst's nonverbal participation with him. The state of the patient's ego integration and differentiation is such that he has not yet developed a durable internalized image of himself, or of the analyst, or both. Until such time in the therapy as his ego functioning has matured further than this, his ability to utilize verbal interpretations is very limited.

The patient's flawed sense of both inner and outer reality tempts the analyst to try to impose upon him what would be only another pseudo-reality and pseudo-identity, and in such an endeavor the analyst would be avoiding, unwittingly, his own full experiencing of the impact upon him of the patient's transference "reality." Of crucial importance is the analyst's becoming able to discern nuclei of reality in the patient's transference images of him.

In particularly difficult cases, the analyst's utilization, while interpreting, of the patient's own customary phraseology and emotional tone may be unusually effective.

The nature of the patient's transference reactions and attitudes to the analyst's interpretations, and to his silences, is important to note and to explore with the patient insofar as feasible.

The analyst is silent in limitless ways which are *in reality* (beyond, that is, the patient's transference-distorted perceptions of these) subtly different. For example, even though he may choose silently to postpone a verbal interpretation of some newly discerned area of conflict in the patient, his nonverbal demeanor toward him is likely to change, nonetheless, in a fashion which helps to prepare the patient, through mutual nonverbal cuing, to become able to utilize, eventually, verbal interpretations concerning this area.

As regards the interpretation of the patient's pathologic identifications, I caution against doing so prematurely in working with these patients, whose sense of an own self is so precariously based. But I point out, on the other hand, the value of coming to explore the successive levels of unconscious identifications which are hidden behind the more nearly conscious levels, such that a more genuine "own self" can eventually come into being in the patient.

The final point in my paper is that the analyst cannot treat the borderline patient effectively if he, the analyst, is unwittingly using the patient to bear the burden of all the severe psychopathology in the whole relationship.

REFERENCES

BERGER, M. M. (Ed.) (1970). *Videotape Techniques in Psychiatric Training and Treatment.* New York: Brunner/Mazel.

DEUTSCH, H. (1942). Some forms of emotional disturbance and their relationship to schizophrenia. *Psychoanal. Quart.*, 11:301-321.

KHAN, M. M. R. (1974). *The Primacy of the Self—Papers on Psychoanalytic Theory and Technique.* New York: International Universities Press.

LICHTENSTEIN, H. (1961). Identity and sexuality: A study of their interrelationship in man. *J. Amer. Psychoanal. Assn.*, 9:179-260. Quotes are from 207-8.

LICHTENSTEIN, H. (1964). The role of narcissism in the emergence and maintenance of a primary identity. *Internat. J. Psycho-Anal.*, 45:49-56.

MAHLER, M. S. (1968). *On Human Symbiosis and the Vicissitudes of Individuation—*Vol. 1*—Infantile Psychosis.* New York: International Universities Press.

MAHLER, M. S., PINE, F., and BERGMAN, A. (1975). *The Psychological Birth of the Human Infant—Symbiosis and Individuation.* New York: Basic Books.

NELSON, M. C., NELSON, B., SHERMAN, M. H., and STREAN, H. S. (1968). *Roles and Paradigms in Psychotherapy.* New York and London: Grune & Stratton.

SCHULZ, C. G. (1952). Comment (unpublished) during staff conference at Chestnut Lodge, Rockville, Maryland.

SEARLES, H. F. (1959). Integration and differentiation in schizophrenia. *J. Nerv. and Ment. Dis.*, 129:542-550. Reprinted on pp. 304-316 in *Collected Papers on Schizophrenia and Related Subjects.* London: Hogarth Press, and New York: International Universities Press, 1965.

SEARLES, H. F. (1965). *Collected Papers on Schizophrenia and Related Subjects.* London: Hogarth Press, and New York: International Universities Press.

SEARLES, H. F. (1970). Autism and the phase of transition to therapeutic symbiosis. *Contemporary Psychoanalysis,* 7:1-20.

SEARLES, H. F. (1971). Pathologic symbiosis and autism. On pp. 69-83 in *In the Name of Life—Essays in Honor of Erich Fromm,* ed. by B. Landis and E. S. Tauber. New York: Holt, Rinehart and Winston.

SEARLES, H. F. (1972). The function of the patient's realistic perceptions of the analyst in delusional transference. *Brit. J. Med. Psychol.,* 45:1-18.

SEARLES, H. F. (1973). Concerning therapeutic symbiosis. *Annual of Psychoanalysis,* 1:247-262.

SEARLES, H. F. (1976). Transitional phenomena and therapeutic symbiosis. *Int. J. Psychoanalytic Psychotherapy,* 5:145-204.

SEARLES, H. F. (1978). (A) Jealousy involving an internal object, and (B) The countertransference in psychoanalytic therapy with borderline patients. To appear in *Stable Instability—Modern Approaches to the Bor-*

derline Syndrome, ed. by J. LeBoit and A. Capponi. New York: Jason Aronson.

SPITZ, R. A. (1957). *No and Yes—On the Genesis of Human Communication*. New York: International Universities Press.

STIERLIN, H. (1959). The adaptation to the "stronger" person's reality—some aspects of the symbiotic relationship of the schizophrenic. *Psychiatry*, 22:143-152.

Discussion

Dr. Giovacchini: When I first read this paper I had considerable difficulty with it. It wasn't really too clear to me what Dr. Searles was trying to get at. Now I am aware of why I had this difficulty. I wonder if some of you might share this. Dr. Searles touches upon many different topics. True, they are related to each other, but each one of them alone would be worth an investigative attempt.

I don't know that I have much to say, since there isn't much here that I fundamentally disagree with. Perhaps I might talk about some change of emphasis. I'm very familiar with many of the clinical situations Dr. Searles refers to. Let me just make some comments about the analyst's having to get into touch, to make contact with, primitive parts of himself so that the patient can effectively project. I certainly would agree with this but I would also add that the analyst, at the same time, must maintain higher levels of organization; otherwise we would have *folie à deux*.

There are also instances where the patient is purposely, unconsciously, but purposely, trying to get the analyst to react with primitive parts of the self, reactions that are not necessarily responses to the patient's projections. Instead the patient is attempting to get responses to specific needs. I will briefly refer to the kind of interaction I'm talking about. These are patients, very primitive patients, who have had extreme difficulty in maintaining a mental representation of me. Their analyses have been punctuated with episodes of apathetic terror, to use an expression of Federn (1952). They felt they would lose me and, in order to be able to hold me, they have to get me to react irrationally or violently. I can recall one patient who succeeded in getting me so angry that I had to throw her out of the consultation room. Then, later, at the end of the day, she called me and said, "Are you all right?" and I said, "Yes, I'm better now," and she was very happy about that because she had succeeded in making me feel as miserable as she felt. At the same time she was able to cathect my external representation and thereby to reinforce the mental representation that she was losing.

Dr. Kernberg: Again I will try to focus on areas of disagreement, although, truly, there are many aspects of the technical, tactical management, session by session, with which I quite strongly agree. My first area of disagreement again has to do with the use of terminology. I am concerned over the tendency all of us seem to have to use different words for the same phenomenon, and the same words for very different phenomena. This applies particularly regarding the use of the terms autism, symbiosis, separation, and individuation. I think that, although Dr. Searles quotes Dr. Mahler, there is a misunderstanding of Mahler in this presentation. Dr. Mahler has very carefully pointed to a sequence of developmental stages which starts out with autism. In fact, I don't know whether, other than in autistic psychosis in childhood, we really see autism in a strict sense. What we see is a kind of secondary autism that has to do with regressive features in the treatment of infantile symbiotic psychosis or adult schizophrenia. This probably warrants the clinical use of the term, but, again, all of these are very regressed psychotic patients.

In my opinion, Dr. Searles is doing an injustice to the impressive clarity that his own use of these terms introduced when years ago he spelled out stages of the differentiation of transferences of psychotic patients. I have learned from Dr. Searles to think of the initial stage of noncontact in the treatment of psychosis as having autistic implications, to be followed by the development of symbiotic, fused stages of the transference (both messianically ecstatic and aggressively determined), and finally by the development of individuation and separation: I understand there to be stages in the transference of psychotic patients. I am disturbed, therefore, to see him use the same terms in talking about borderline patients who have different kinds of transference—and where I have never seen autistic phenomena, and very rarely symbiotic ones. Dr. Mahler has stressed that it is in the rapprochement subphase of separation-individuation within her developmental scheme that borderline pathology develops, and I think she gives very good evidence for that in her theoretical and clinical writings.

But the way Dr. Searles uses this terminology makes me wonder to what extent he has revised his earlier thinking, or is using terms that I have come to associate in recent years with Mahler in radically different ways. It is true that border-line patients have a confused sense of identity, but that does not mean that they have a fusion of their identity with that of the analyst. It means that they have a lack of integration of contradictory aspects of their self-images or self-representations. Thus, we have to differentiate patients who don't have a sense of identity because they experience fusion phenomena (they live in a symbiotic relation) from those patients who present a very good and sharp differentiation between self- and object representation, but lack integration of them. These latter ones are borderline patients.

Regarding clinical issues, Dr. Searles stresses the importance of focusing on the nonverbal aspects of the interaction. I fully agree that this is extremely important. I don't see the importance of the focus on the total emotional atmosphere of the psychotherapeutic setting as being in contradiction to a focus on the interpretations. To the contrary—and here we disagree sharply—it seems to me that an interpretive approach can be extremely helpful from the beginning of the treatment. Again, in partial agreement with him, I think that to interpret isolated dreams or isolated genetic elements leads into never-never land. But to interpret systematically the unconscious implications of the "here and now" interactions is a crucial interpretive tool within an atmosphere of technical neutrality. I think the dangers to which he points are very real; for example, if our interpretations insist of the reality the patient has denied, the patient may experience them as a powerful invasion or brainwashing. But Dr. Searles himself has pointed out that one can interpret the patient's interpretation of our therapeutic interventions (his experiencing the therapist as "brainwashing"). In general, to interpret the patient's interpretations of our interpretations is a key aspect, it seems to me, of an essentially analytic approach to borderline patients that protects our interpretations from regressive distortions in the transference.

Regarding silence, I fully agree that there are many meanings of silence. I'm concerned about the idealization of nonverbal communication. Borderline patients are often extremely keen to interpret little details, while blandly and bluntly neglecting dominant realities. If one becomes overcautious, overconcerned about details and neglects the most overriding and important issues in the transference, one feeds into the patient's omnipotent control. I would be very concerned about an analyst who spent 80 to 90 percent of his time in silence with borderline patients. I find myself intervening quite actively from the beginning of the treatment, but that doesn't mean that I don't intervene from a position of technical neutrality.

Finally, I think that while it is very important to examine within oneself the countertransference issues, it is equally important to avoid an idealization of countertransference. Here I agree with Dr. Giovacchini: It is hoped that we don't have the same pathology that our patients have and, yet, we should have the capacity for empathy with all kinds of human feelings and pathology. But, although it sometimes unfortunately happens that a therapist has problems similar to those of a patient of his, it is hoped this happens in a very minor, restricted situation; otherwise, I think it would seriously interfere with his internal freedom to help the patient in his own terms, and could feed into the patient's efforts to convince the therapist that he is as sick as the patient. That kind of symmetrical relationship of patient and therapist is often a consequence of the patient's unconscious efforts to make the treatment interminable, or to perpetuate his pathological frame of reference regarding treatment and life in general.

Dr. Masterson: Dr. Searles has for years been informing us with his knowledge, as he has entertained us with his style. His emphasis on the extraordinarily complex and minute shifts of affect in both patient and therapist and how they affect the course of psychotherapy has given him a unique and lasting position in the field. He has done it again today in his own inimitable way. His reflective paper touches on many aspects of therapy which we have all probably given some thought to before but perhaps not so deeply. I found myself in accord with a great deal that he has said about therapy.

However, given all this, there was one aspect of the paper which, in the context of today's subject, the borderline, might give rise to substantial confusion. The confusion lies, in my judgment, with Dr. Searles having too broad a definition of the borderline patient. He states that the ego functioning of the patients he is referring to is autistic. Their biggest problems are the perception of reality, both inner and outer. In my judgment this makes these patients clearly psychotic and not borderline and, therefore, suggests that their therapeutic needs are different from those of the borderline and so they require some differences in therapeutic technique. In developmental terms they are fixated at the symbiotic level or earlier so that their therapeutic need is to be able to establish and maintain a symbiotic tie with the therapist and not, as in the borderline, to resolve that tie. They do not have a consensual perception of reality against which to measure the therapist's confrontations. Dr. Searles suggests that these techniques could lead to the patient's becoming the object of the analyst. Perhaps with psychotic patients his contentions are quite valid.

However, how does the borderline differ from the psychotic so that techniques that would be disastrous for the one are useful for the other? The borderline has separated from the symbiotic relationship with the mother and is fixated at this stage of separation-individuation. Though the borderline has some difficulty with reality perception, his chief problem is not an inability to perceive reality but the need to deny the reality he does perceive in order to foster the externalization and acting-out of his past and present. As I mentioned in my discussion of Dr. Giovacchini's paper, this externalization and acting-out must be dealt with before the patient becomes aware that the problem exists in his psyche and comes from the past rather than exists in the environment and comes from the present.

———————

Dr. Searles: When Dr. Kernberg says that among borderline patients we never see autistic ones and very rarely symbiotic ones, I don't get it. I don't understand it. As to all this about terminology—I acknowledge that after spending nearly 15 years working with patients at Chestnut Lodge—very, very psychotic most of them, very chronically psychotic people—I am conscious of a need in myself to find that that experience is relevant to less ill people. I have a personal need to see it as relevant. But even if I discount most generously for that personal need of mine, I am impressed with the relevancy of that Chestnut Lodge experience in my daily work with patients whom I regard as borderline or schizoid. I am remarkably struck by the essentially qualitative likeness of the phenomena I'm encountering, these days, to those I encountered in working with the chronically psychotic patients. And, of course, I share Dr. Kernberg's statement that empathy is of the essence—that we need to be empathic with our patients—but to my mind that empathy necessarily requires that we be in touch with some comparable experience in our own developmental history—something comparable to what we see in the patient before us. That is the basis for our empathy, and saying this is not, in my way of thinking, any glorification of illness, not at all. This has been one of my main sources of unfriendliness toward the classically analytic position, and I have been through the mill with the classical analytic thing. And when I speak about the regrettable aspect of burdening the patient with all of the severe psychopathology in the relationship, I know from where I speak. It is a real disservice to the patient to disclaim that one possesses in oneself something of essentially the same nature. This is the kind of point that I was trying to make.

REFERENCE

FEDERN, P. (1952). *Ego Psychology and the Psychoses.* New York: Basic Books.

Chapter 3

Contrasting Approaches

to the Psychotherapy

of Borderline Conditions

Otto F. Kernberg, M.D.

In this paper, I focus on issues pertaining to the psychoanalytic psychotherapy of borderline conditions. I shall start out with an effort to outline a theory of psychoanalytic psychotherapy and summarize briefly my own approach to borderline patients within this theoretical frame and then examine critically some alternative psychoanalytic psychotherapeutic approaches to borderline conditions. Finally, I shall attempt to illustrate transference developments in the psychoanalytic psychotherapy of a borderline patient during the third year of treatment.

1. REVIEW OF THE THEORY OF PSYCHOANALYTIC PSYCHOTHERAPY

Classical psychoanalytic theory of psychopathology conceives of symptom formation as a compromise solution between repressed, unconscious instinctual urges and defense mechanisms operating against them. The essential theory of therapeutic change by means of psychoanalysis focuses on the resolution of unconscious conflict (between instinctual

urges and defensive constellations) by means of interpretation of the defenses (and their motives) that are manifest as
resistances to free association in the analytic situation. Resolution of resistances, and, in this context, gradual emergence,
interpretation, and integration of unconscious impulses are the
core tasks of psychoanalytic treatment.

Throughout psychoanalytic treatment, the primary manifestations of both impulses and defenses occur in the transference. Following Gill's suggestion (1954), psychoanalysis
may be defined as the establishment of a therapeutic setting
that permits the development of a regressive transference
neurosis solely by means of interpretation, carried out by the
analyst from a position of technical neutrality.

There are two important implications for a theory of
psychoanalytic psychotherapy in this definition. First, if psychoanalysis is defined by 1) a position of technical neutrality,
2) the predominant use of interpretation as a major psychotherapeutic tool, and 3) the systematic analysis of the transference, psychoanalytic psychotherapies may be defined in
terms of changes or modification in any or all of these three
technical paradigms. In fact, I think the definition of a spectrum of psychoanalytic psychotherapies, ranging from psychoanalysis, on the one extreme, to supportive psychotherapies on the other, is still possible in terms of these three basic
paradigms. Second, it needs to be stressed that the analysis of
the transference involves, simultaneously, the analysis of instinctual urges and defenses against them, and of particular
object relations (within which these instinctual urges and
defenses against them are played out).

Within an ego-psychological approach, psychoanalytic
psychotherapy may be defined as a psychoanalytically based

or oriented treatment that does not attempt, as its goal, a systematic resolution of unconscious conflicts and, therefore, of all impulse/defense configurations and the respective resistances; rather, it attempts a partial resolution of some, and a reinforcement of other resistances, with a subsequent, partial integration of previously repressed impulses into the adult ego. As a result, a partial increase of ego strength and flexibility may take place, which then permits a more effective repression of residual, dynamically unconscious impulses, and a modified impulse/defense configuration (that increases the adaptive—in contrast to maladaptive—aspects of character formation). This definition differentiates psychoanalysis from psychoanalytic psychotherapy, both in the goals and in the underlying theory of change reflected in these differential goals.

Regarding the techniques employed in psychoanalytic psychotherapy geared to the achievement of those goals, and the differences between such techniques and those of psychoanalysis proper, the ego-psychological approach defines three major modalities of treatment based upon the psychoanalytic framework: 1) exploratory, insight, uncovering, or, simply, expressive psychoanalytic psychotherapy; 2) suppressive or supportive psychotherapy; and 3) counseling and other related, "non-dynamic" psychotherapies.

Expressive psychotherapy is characterized by the utilization of clarification and interpretation as major tools, and, in this context, also abreaction. Partial aspects of the transference are interpreted, and the therapist actively selects such transferences to be interpreted in the light of the particular goals of treatment, the predominant transference resistances, and the patient's external reality. Technical neutrality is usually maintained, but a systematic analysis of all transference paradigms or a systematic resolution of the transference neurosis by interpretation alone is definitely not attempted.

Supportive psychotherapy is characterized by partial use of clarification and abreaction, and the predominance of the use of the technical tools of suggestion and manipulation. Bibring (1954) defined these techniques and illustrated their technical utilization. Insofar as supportive psychotherapy still implies an acute awareness and monitoring of the transference on the part of the psychotherapist, and a careful consideration of transference resistances as part of his overall technique in dealing with characterological problems and their connection to the patient's life difficulties, this is still a psychoanalytic psychotherapy in a broad sense. By definition, however, transference is not interpreted in purely supportive psychotherapy, and the utilization of technical tools such as suggestion and manipulation implicitly eliminates technical neutrality.

Counseling and other psychotherapies that focus exclusively on conscious, cognitive and/or affective issues may be defined as supportive psychotherapies that do not include a consideration of transference processes on the part of the psychotherapist.

The major problem with this psychoanalytic theory and technique of psychoanalytic psychotherapy has been the contradiction between the theoretical model from which it stems and the structural intrapsychic organization of many patients with whom it has been used. The theoretical model underlying this approach holds remarkably well for patients with good ego strength. In contrast, however, the application of this psychoanalytic psychotherapy model to patients with severe psychopathologies—particularly the borderline conditions—has led to puzzling and contradictory findings.

First, these patients present a constellation of primitive defensive mechanisms centering around dissociation of contradictory ego states rather than on repression. Second, the transferences of these patients have peculiarities that are very different from the more usual transference developments in better functioning patients. Third, and most importantly, their primitive impulses are not unconscious but mutually dissociated in consciousness. In this connection, the evaluation of defense-impulse constellations often does not permit a clarification of what agency within the tripartite structure (ego, superego, and id) is motivating and activating a defense against what impulse within what other agency. In other words, the transference seems to reflect contradictory ego states that incorporate contradictory, primitive internalized object relations within an overall psychic matrix that does not present a clear differentiation of ego, superego and id.

This leads to an additional, specialized psychoanalytic approach that attempts to deal with the phenomena just described, namely, psychoanalytic object relations theory.

Within an object relations framework, intrapsychic conflicts are conceptualized as always involving self- and object representations, or, rather, as conflicts between certain units of self- and object representations under the impact of a determined drive derivative (clinically, a certain affect disposition) and other, contradictory or opposite units of self- and object representations under the impact of their respective affect dispositions. Unconscious intrapsychic conflicts are never simply conflicts between impulse and defense, but, rather, the drive derivative is represented by a certain primitive ob-

ject relation (a certain unit of self- and object representation), and the defense, as well, is reflected by a certain
internalized object relation. Thus, all character defenses really
reflect the activation of a defensive constellation of self- and
object representations directed against an opposite and
dreaded, repressed self-object constellation. For example, in
obsessive, characterological submissiveness, a chronically sub-
missive self-image in relating to a powerful and protective
oedipal parental image may defend the patient against the
repressed, violently rebellious self relating to a sadistic and
controlling parental image. Thus, clinically, both character
defenses and repressed impulses involve mutually opposed
internal object relations.

From the viewpoint of object relations theory, the consolidation of the overall intrapsychic structures (ego, superego and id) results in an integration of internalized object
relations that obscures the constituent self representation-
object representation-affect units within the overall structural
properties of the tripartite system (Kernberg, 1976a); the
psychopathology of the symptomatic neuroses and less severe
character neuroses is produced by intersystemic conflicts between such integrated ego, superego and id systems. In contrast, in the psychopathology of borderline personality organization, such an integration of the major intrapsychic agencies
is not achieved, and conflicts are, therefore, largely or mostly
intrasystemic (within an undifferentiated ego-id matrix). In
severe psychopathologies—particularly the borderline conditions—early, primitive units of internalized object relations
are directly manifest in the transference, in the context of
mutually conflictual drive derivatives reflected in contradictory ego states.

In these cases, the predominance of a constellation of early defense mechanisms centering around primitive dissociation or splitting immediately activates, in the transference, mutually contradictory, primitive but conscious intrapsychic conflicts (Kernberg, 1975). What appears on the surface as inappropriate, primitive, chaotic character traits and inter-personal interactions, impulsive behavior and affect storms actually reflect the fantastic, early object relations derived structures that are the building blocks of the later tripartite system. These object relations determine the characteristics of primitive transferences, that is, of highly fantastic, unreal precipitates of early object relations that do not reflect directly the real object relations of infancy and childhood, and that have to be interpreted integratively until, by recon-stitution of total—in contrast to partial or split—object rela-tions, the more real aspects of the developmental history emerge (Kernberg, 1976b). In the treatment, structural inte-gration through interpretation precedes genetic reconstruc-tions.

Let me now spell out a proposal for an integration of ego psychological and object relations theory derived concep-tualizations geared to outlining a theory of psychoanalytic psychotherapy.

For patients with good ego strength, the definition of psy-choanalytic psychotherapy as originally proposed by ego psy-chological authors (Bibring, 1954; Gill, 1954) still stands; and so does the possibility of gradual transition between expressive and supportive techniques, and the effectiveness of supportive techniques themselves for such cases. The three paradigms—1) the predominant technical tools (clarification and interpretation versus suggestion and manipulation), 2) the extent to which a systematic working through a full-fledged transference neurosis is attempted and achieved, and 3) the degree to which technical neutrality is maintained—jointly define the predominant nature of the psychotherapy within the expressive-supportive continuum.

In cases with severe psychopathology—typically, the borderline conditions—the characteristics of psychoanalytic psychotherapy can no longer be defined as similar to those for patients with well integrated tripartite structure, and require a new set of definitions. Maintaining the three basic paradigms along which differentiation of psychoanalysis proper from psychoanalytic psychotherapy can be established, here psychoanalytic psychotherapy might be described as follows.

Because primitive transferences are immediately available, predominate as resistances, and, in fact, determine the severity of intrapsychic and interpersonal disturbances, they can and need to be focused upon immediately, starting out from their interpretation only in the "here and now," and leading into genetic reconstructions only at late stages of the treatment (when primitive transferences determined by part object relations have been transformed into advanced transferences or total object relations, thus approaching the more realistic experiences of childhood that lend themselves to genetic reconstruction). Interpretation of the transference requires that the therapist maintain a position of technical neutrality for the reason that there can be no interpretation of primitive transferences without a firm, consistent, stable maintenance of reality boundaries in the therapeutic situation, and without an active caution on the part of the therapist not to be "sucked into" the reactivation of pathological primitive object relations by the patient. Insofar as both transference interpretation and a position of technical neutrality require the use of clarification and interpretation and contraindicate the use of suggestive and manipulative techniques, clarification and the interpretation are maintained as principal techniques.

However, in contrast to psychoanalysis proper, transference interpretation is not systematic. Because there is a need to focus on the severity of acting-out and on the disturbances in the patient's external reality (that may threaten the continuity of the treatment as well as the patient's psychosocial survival) and, also, because, as part of acting-out of primitive transferences, the treatment easily comes to replace life, transference interpretation now has to be codetermined by: 1) the predominant transference paradigm, 2) the prevailing conflicts in immediate reality, and 3) the overall, specific goals of treatment. In addition, technical neutrality is limited by the need to establish parameters of technique, including, in certain cases, the structuring of the patient's external life and the establishment of a teamwork approach with patients who cannot function autonomously during long stretches of their psychotherapy. Technical neutrality, therefore, is a theoretical baseline from which deviations occur again and again, to be reduced—again and again—by interpretation. One crucial aspect of psychoanalytic psychotherapy with patients presenting severe psychopathology is the systematic interpretation of defenses. In contrast to expressive psychotherapies in better functioning patients—where certain defenses are selectively interpreted while others are not touched—the systematic interpretation of defenses in severe psychopathology is crucial to improve ego functioning and to permit the transformation and resolution of primitive transferences.

Therefore, the similarity between expressive psychoanalytic

psychotherapy and psychoanalysis is greater in the case of severe psychopathology than in the case of patients with milder psychological illness. One might say that, in psycho-analytic psychotherapy of borderline conditions, the tactical approach to each session may be almost indistinguishable from psychoanalysis proper, and that only from a long-term, strate-gic viewpoint do the differences between psychoanalysis proper and psychoanalytic psychotherapy emerge. By the same token, the cleavage between expressive psychotherapy and supportive psychotherapy is sharp and definite in the case of patients with borderline conditions, while it is more gradual and blurred in cases with less severe illness. In other words, it is not possible to bring about significant personality modifica-tions by means of psychoanalytic psychotherapy in patients with severe psychopathology without exploration and resolu-tion of primitive transferences, and this requires a purely expressive, meticulously analytic approach, although not psy-choanalysis proper. I think it is important to maintain a care-ful distinction between psychoanalytic psychotherapy and psychoanalysis in all cases; however, space does not permit me to go into the reasons for this conviction here. There are, undoubtedly, important supportive effects inherent in such a purely expressive approach, but one has to differentiate sharply supportive effects from supportive techniques, an issue that requires more elaboration than is possible in this overview.

There is one more theoretical paradigm along which psy-choanalytic psychotherapy of severely regressed patients needs to be defined. This relates to the focus on the degree of differentiation of self- and object representations in types of psychopathology characterized by fixation or regression to developmental levels preceding object constancy. In a schematic summary of the degree of self-object differentiation within such a developmental continuum, the following spectrum of regressive pathology may be described.

First, we have the regression to psychotic identifications in Jacobson's (1954) terms or the symbiotic stage of development in Mahler's terms (1968), in which the differentiation between self and non-self is abolished and self- and object representations re-fuse: Here we find only idealized, ecstatic merged states, and terrifying, aggressive merged stages. The main emphasis in such cases has to be on gradually helping the patient to differentiate his internal life from the therapist's psychological reality, on stressing the reality of the immediate therapeutic interaction, and on being alert to the dangers in the patient's life derived from the breakdown of ego boundaries outside the therapeutic situation. It seems to me that Searles' work with schizophrenic patients (1965) speaks to this point.

Second, there are patients in whom the regression has occurred to a stage of differentiation preceding the typical borderline pathology (reflected in splitting of good and bad self- and object representations), but more advanced than that of psychotic refusion. Usually, these are patients with predominant schizoid characteristics, and one may find such developments from early on in the treatment of some schizoid personalities. Here, the prevailing level of regression or fixation relates to the early differentiation subphase of the stage of separation-individuation where patients require "holding" (Winnicott, 1965), being empathized with and yet permitted to maintain their autonomy vis-à-vis the therapist. A temporary regressive state reflecting this development may signify a potential for new ego growth, as Balint (1968) and Winnicott (1958, 1965) have suggested. It is very important, however, to differentiate these regressive developments from more malignant regression to "preverbal" blurring of defensive constellations characteristic of some borderline patients, a defensive destruction of verbal communication, where the predominant issues are precisely the working through of primitive defensive operations, object relations, and oedipalized aggression. In other words, I think that an overgeneralization of Balint's and Winnicott's approaches can seriously play into patients' defensive needs to omnipotently control the therapist and destroy the therapeutic situation by means of "preverbal" regressive features.

Third, the next level of regressive development is precisely that typical of borderline personality organization. Here the problem is no longer the need to protect the gradually emerging autonomous self of the differentiation subphase of separation-individuation, but rather, the integration of mutually split-off aspects of self- and object representations reflecting pathology for the most part linked—as Mahler found—with the rapprochement subphase (1971, 1972). In other words, in these patients, the issue is not between autonomy or merger, or between true and false self, but between non-integrated and integrated self, non-integrated and integrated object relations.

In earlier work (1975, 1976a, 1976b), I have outlined a technical approach to borderline patients that can be briefly summarized as follows: First, the dissociated or generally fragmented aspects of the patient's intrapsychic conflicts are gradually integrated into significant units of primitive internalized object relations. Second, each unit (constituted of a particular self-image, a particular object image, and a major affect disposition linking these) then needs to be clarified as it becomes activated in the transference, including the alternation of reciprocal self- and object re-enactments in the relationship with the therapist. Third, when these units can be interpreted and integrated with other related or contradictory units—particularly when libidinally invested and aggressively invested units can be integrated—the process of working-through of the transference and of the resolution of primitive constellations of defensive operations characteristic of borderline conditions has begun.

2. A Critical Review of Some Alternative Approaches to the Psychoanalytic Psychotherapy of Borderline Conditions

Within the British object relations orientation, Little's (1957, 1960, 1966) and Winnicott's (1958, 1965) contributions to the psychoanalytic psychotherapy of borderline patients are continuing to have important influence. Little's work focuses mostly on technique. Although she assumes that the patients she describes are mostly borderline conditions, her implication that her patients presented a lack of differentiation between self and object, and her technical proposals for helping them develop a sense of uniqueness and separateness, seem to focus on the pathology of the early differentiation subphase of separation-individuation. Her views are somewhat related to those of Balint and Winnicott, but her patients seem to be more regressed than those described by these two authors. In this connection, Winnicott (1960) stressed the need to permit the patient to develop his "true self" by avoiding an "impingement" upon him at certain stages of therapeutic regression; this focus may also reflect an emphasis on the pathology of the developmental subphase of differentiation of separation-individuation, a relatively earlier one than that connected with borderline conditions in Mahler's and my own work.

Bion's (1965, 1967, 1970) writings are difficult to classify from the viewpoint of this outline. One technical aspect of his contributions to the treatment of severely regressed patients is the conception of the analyst as a "container," which reflects, in my opinion, a cognitive counterpart to Winnicott's focus on the "holding" function of the psychoanalyst. Bion's latest writings, particularly the Brazilian lectures (1974, 1975, 1977), consist of formulations that combine, on the one hand, a refreshing (one might also say long overdue) critique of authoritarian formulations of interpretations on the basis of the analyst's preconceived theories (apparently a stab in the direction of his Kleinian colleagues), and, on the other hand, an emotionally charged attitude, a religious-mythical atmosphere, which seems uncomfortably directed against an objective psychoanalytic method and approach.

In the United States, Zetzel (1971) and Grinker (1975) seem to be the last proponents of the purely supportive approach to the psychotherapy of borderline conditions that was so fashionable 20 years ago. I have criticized a supportive approach to borderline conditions in earlier work (Kernberg et al., 1972; Kernberg, 1975), and the first section of this paper synthesizes my theoretical frame regarding this issue. However, the fear expressed in earlier literature regarding the presumed "frailty" of the defensive system, personality organization, and transferences of borderline conditions is still reflected in various psychoanalytically based but operationally manipulative approaches, such as those of Marie Nelson (1967) and Arlene Wolberg (1973). Nelson's "paradigmatic psychotherapy" attempts to evolve techniques that circumvent borderline patients' resistances, and Wolberg utilizes "projective therapeutic techniques" in examining the patient's intrapsychic problems as if they were the problems of other people with whom the patient relates (thus accepting the patient's projections rather than interpreting them).

I have already expressed my strong criticism of the attempts to combine manipulative or suggestive maneuvers with an interpretive approach to borderline conditions. Manipulative or suggestive techniques destroy technical neutrality and interfere with the possibility of analyzing primitive transferences and resistances. Such analysis is the most important ego strengthening aspect of the psychoanalytic psychotherapy of borderline patients. In this connection, there are several current, rather widespread misunderstandings regarding the nature of supportive interventions and the functions of empathy and confrontation in the early stages—or throughout the entire course of treatment of borderline conditions.

Technical neutrality means equidistance from the forces codetermining the patient's intrapsychic conflicts, and not lack of warmth or empathy with him. One still hears comments implying that borderline patients need, first of all, empathic understanding rather than a precise theory and cognitively sharpened interpretations based on such a theory. All psychotherapy requires as a base line the therapist's capacity for authentic human warmth and empathy; these qualities are preconditions for any appropriate psychotherapeutic work.

Empathy, however, is not only the intuitive, emotional awareness in the therapist of the patient's central emotional experience at a certain point, but must also include the therapist's
capacity to empathize with that which the patient can not
tolerate within himself; therefore, therapeutic empathy tran-
scends the empathy involved in ordinary human interactions,
and includes the therapist's integration, on a cognitive and
emotional level, of what is actively dissociated or split in borderline patients. It is very important for the therapist working
with borderline patients to be able to integrate both cognitive
and emotional aspects in his understanding of the therapeutic
situation, and the idealization of either the cognitive ("containing") or the emotional ("holding") as opposed to each
other, seriously limits a psychoanalytic psychotherapeutic
approach with borderline cases.

In addition, when serious distortions in the patient's reality
testing in the psychotherapeutic hours evolve as part of the
activation of primitive transferences and primitive defensive
operations (particularly that of projective identification), it
may be crucial for the therapist to start out his interpretive
efforts by clarifying the reality of the therapeutic situation.
Such initial interventions often require a great deal of active
work on the part of the therapist, a direct dealing with what
the reality is in the sessions or in the patient's external life,
that may be misunderstood as a technically supportive, suggestive, or manipulative intervention.

This brings me to the review of Masterson's (1972, 1976)
recent contributions, particularly his proposal that psychotherapy with borderline patients starts out as supportive
psychotherapy and that intensive reconstructive psychoanalytically oriented psychotherapy is usually an expansion and

outgrowth of supportive psychotherapy. It seems to me that Masterson's general approach is quite close to mine. He stresses the importance of the analysis of primitive transferences, and has expanded on the description of two mutually split off part object relations units—the rewarding or libidinal part object relations unit and the withdrawing or aggressive part object relations unit—thus combining an object relations viewpoint with a developmental model based upon Mahler's work. However, what Masterson describes as the early, supportive stage of the treatment is probably the kind of structuring of the treatment situation and clarification and confrontation of the early manifestations of primitive defensive operations in the psychotherapeutic setting that I would consider part of an essentially analytic approach. Here, his term "supportive" may refer more to the effect than to the techniques of treatment, and I think his approach would gain in internal consistency if he clarified this issue. One other reservation regarding his treatment approach concerns the relative simplifications of primitive transferences in the two part object relations units mentioned: I think one sees much more complex—both more fragmented and more integrative— aspects of self- and object representations in borderline patients, as well as more pathological condensation of preoedipal and oedipal object relations, than seem to be reflected in his cases.

Rinsley (1977) and Furer (1977) are other authors among a growing group of psychoanalytically oriented therapists who are combining an ego-psychological object relations theory with a developmental model stemming from Mahler's work (Mahler and Kaplan, 1977). Giovacchini (1975), Bergeret (1970), André Green (1975, 1977), Volkan (1975), and Searles (1977) have also been applying object relations theory derived models, and Searles, particularly, has made fundamental contributions to our understanding of the characteristics of transference and countertransference developments in the treatment of borderline and psychotic patients. Comprehensive overviews of some of these approaches can be found in Hartocollis' recent book (1977).

At this point, I would attempt, within the overall theory of technique outlined before, the following synthesis of the recent trends and developments in the psychoanalytic psychotherapy of borderline patients. The analysis of the transference is the central element in the psychoanalytic psychotherapy of borderline patients. In contrast to the systematic analysis of transference paradigms leading to an ordered sequence of working-through of the transference neurosis in the standard psychoanalytic situation of patients with good ego strength, it is the systematic analysis of primitive object relations and defensive operations of borderline conditions, rather than the systematic analysis of their transferences per se, that gives continuity to the therapeutic strategy. The primitive nature of the transference of borderline patients requires an expansion of the technical approach to the treatment situation along the following lines.

First, insofar as the tripartite intrapsychic structures have not fully consolidated in these cases, the interpretation of impulse-defense configurations cannot be carried out within a frame of intersystemic conflicts, except in advanced stages of the treatment. Therefore, while an ego-psychological structural approach to unconscious intrapsychic conflicts is crucial to understanding these patients, the standard structural approach needs to be amplified with an object relations and a developmental approach. The object relations approach permits the analysis of the moment-to-moment variations of the transference in terms of the activation of units of self- and object representations, including the analysis of the alternating reciprocal activation of self- and object representations in the patient/therapist dyad.

Second, insofar as early developmental stages may be reactivated, implying a decrease in the ordinary predominance of symbolic communication by verbal means, the analysis of the total behavior of the patient within the therapeutic setting may take precedence temporarily over the analysis of verbal communication per se.

Third, insofar as these patients, by definition, present identity diffusion (and, therefore, a lack of an integrated self that relates to integrated object representations and is able to conceive realistically of integrated external objects), the therapist needs to explore the immediate emotional relationship between himself and the patient with an attempt toward the intrapsychic integration within the therapist (by emotional and cognitive integrative processes) of the part object relations world reflected in the transference. In other words, the intrapsychic "space" of the therapist becomes the diagnostic instrument that analyzes the therapeutic relation at such points. The therapist's internal integrative efforts and, with them, his total emotional reaction to the patient (including his countertransference in a strict sense) acquire a predominant function.

Fourth, insofar as the activation of preverbal and early verbal stages of development are reflected in the patient's behavior in relation to the total treatment situation, the therapist's focus on the psychotherapeutic "setting" complements his focus on his intrapsychic, integrative efforts and on his ordinary understanding of verbal communications in the therapy situation.

In short, in contrast to the standard psychoanalytic situation, here the therapist's instruments for analysis of the transference include a larger focus on the psychotherapeutic setting, on his emotional response, and a relatively more restricted focus on the patient's free associations or general verbal communication per se.

Among the principal dangers confronting the therapist under these conditions are: 1) transference acting-out requiring external structure and/or structuring in the therapeutic situation itself, temporarily limiting technical neutrality and, by the same token, the possibility of interpretive work; 2) genetic reductionism, in the sense of premature interpretation of the transference in terms of its developmental implications, thus neglecting the interpretation of complex condensations of preoedipal and oedipal material, and risking a premature deflection of the transference onto its presumed origin; 3) an almost exclusive focus on the "here and now," derived from the need to focus sharply on the moment-to-moment transference changes and the relative lack of availability of solid knowledge of the patient's external reality and his past —this may lead to mystification of the therapeutic interaction, the therapeutic setting, and the therapist's functions; and 4) an exaggerated focus on the countertransference, derived from the importance of the analysis of the therapist's emotional reactions in the treatment with borderline patients: Countertransference acting- out, and feeding into the patient's wishes for a symmetrical nature of the therapeutic relationship can thus be fostered, and the therapist may unwittingly slip into the role of a magic object or into experiencing the patient as essential to the therapist's own emotional well-being.

3. A CASE ILLUSTRATION

The case is that of a woman lawyer in her early thirties, presenting borderline personality organization with predominant masochistic and schizoid features. I saw her in psychoanalytic psychotherapy, three times a week.

In the third year of treatment, after interpretation of primitive defensive operations in the context of condensation of oedipal and preoedipal material centering around her masochistic search for a warm and giving, but also powerful and sadistic, father who would harm her in intercourse, the following transference pattern emerged. She now experienced her oedipal and preoedipal mother combined as a powerful force preventing her from any further improvement. Vague and imprecise speech, serious blocking in the hours with a sense of futility, unending demands for demonstrations of my motherly love and interest, and accusation of me as being cold and rejecting (that is, mother attacking her internally and externally) alternated with sexualized transference reactions in which she experienced me as a sexually exciting but dangerous and powerful man who frightened her. The oedipal qualities of the material became stronger, in the context of an integration of the transference that seemed to reflect more realistic aspects of her childhood, while the conflict between her wishes for a sexual relation with a powerful father and her fear of the punishment from the oedipal mother acquired intersystematic qualities. That is, her mother introject became more and more coincidental with broader superego features, and the intrapsychic conflicts were now intersystemic, in contrast to the previous predominance of chaotic and conscious conflicts among mutually dissociated aspects of the relations with both parents. She also established, for the first time, a sexual relation with a boyfriend, but eventually attempted to escape from the relationship out of an unconscious sense of guilt. Interestingly, she experienced her boyfriend as rather passive and sexually non-threatening and at first found this helpful, but then she perceived his lack of capacity to stand up against the forces in her that tended to destroy a good sexual relationship (her mother introject) as disappointing.

At this point, in the middle of my interpreting the patient's fears of sexual longings for me as father (because they were forbidden by her internal mother) a relatively sudden deterioration occurred, and over a period of several weeks the patient seemed to regress to what had characterized the early stages of her treatment. She now presented an almost disorganized verbal communication (at the beginning of treatment she had presented what almost amounted to a formal disorganization of thought processes), an incapacity to listen to what I was saying, and a growing sense that my understanding of her was terribly incomplete, imperfect and arbitrary. For the first time in her treatment, she expressed a strong wish to shift to another, presumably warmer and more understanding therapist. Efforts to interpret these feelings as a regressive escape from the oedipal aspects of the tranference led nowhere.

At one point, the patient communicated to me quite clearly the wish that I should say only perfect and precise things that would immediately and clearly reflect how she was feeling and reassure her that I was really with her. Otherwise, I should not say anything, and, to the contrary, should listen patiently to her attacks on me. At times, it became practically impossible for me to get a word in, because the patient would interrupt me and distort almost everything that I was saying. I finally did sit back, over several sessions, listening to her lengthy attacks on me, while attempting to gain more understanding of the situation.

I now limited myself to pointing out to her that I understood that she had a great need for me to say the right things, to reassure her, to give her indications that I understood her almost without her having to say anything. Also, I pointed out that I understood that she was terribly afraid that, very easily, anything that I might say was trying to overpower, dominate or brainwash her. After I would say something like this, the patient would sit back as if expecting me to say more, but I didn't. Then she would smile, which I interpreted in my mind as her acknowledgment that I was not attempting to control her and say anything beyond my acknowledgment of this immediate situation.

I must stress that in the early stages of this development I had intended to interpret the patient's attitude as an effort at omnipotent control of me, and the patient's identification with her sadistically perceived mother. That is, I had earlier interpreted her attitude toward me as a reflection of the attitude of her internalized mother (her superego) toward herself (represented by me). But at this stage, any such efforts at interpretation would typically exacerbate the situation and not be helpful at all (in contrast to similar interventions that had been very helpful months earlier). Surprisingly, after several weeks of not doing anything beyond verbalizing the immediate relationship between us as I saw it, the patient felt better, reassured, and had again very positive feelings with sexual implications toward me. However, my efforts to investigate the relationship between these two types of session (those in which she could not take anything from me and had to take over, and those in which she seemed more positive but afraid of her sexual feelings) again led to stalemate.

After some further weeks, I finally formulated the interpretation that she was enacting two alternative relations with me: one in which I was like a warm and receptive, understanding and not controlling mother, and the other, in which I was again a father figure, sexually tempting and dangerous. The patient now said that, when I interpreted her behavior, she saw me as harsh, masculine, invasive, and when I sat back and just listened to her she saw me as soft, feminine, somewhat depressed, and there was something very soothing about it. She said that when she felt understood by me in that way—as a soothing, feminine, depressed person—she could again, later on, listen to me, although I then "made the mistake" of again becoming a masculine and controlling figure.

I now interpreted her double split of me (as masculine and feminine, and good and bad) as an effort to avoid the conflict between the need for a good, warm relation with a mother who could understand and give her love—but who also forbade sex with father, and the need to be a receptive feminine woman to a masculine man standing for a father able to "penetrate" her in spite of her acting as if she rejected him (but, by the same token, threatening her relation with mother). I also interpreted her "getting stuck" in that situation as reflecting a condensation with a very early relationship with her mother, probably stemming from the second or third year of life, in which she felt that her mother could only listen to her when mother was depressed and listless, while any active interest of her mother seemed like an intolerable control and dominance. I added that this reflected one more, deep reason for her incapacity to shift into a dependent relation toward a man who, at the same time, would be sexually attractive to her: Not having the security of a basic acceptance and love by mother who also respected her autonomy, she felt she could not tolerate her sexual feelings for her father.

Months later, I was able to point out to her that her perception of her father as a cruel, controlling, and sexually aggressive man represented a condensation of his masculinity and these qualities of dominance displaced from mother onto him. The patient could now integrate these understandings, and the treatment continued to advance in the direction of further work on her oedipal conflicts.

This brief vignette illustrates how, in an advanced stage of a psychoanalytic psychotherapy with a borderline patient (after years of working through primitive defensive mechanisms and object relations in the transference), a gradual predominance of oedipal conflicts occurred—simultaneously with a shift toward intersystemic conflicts. However, there was, at the same time, a regressive shift toward a very early stage of separation-individuation from mother that required a temporary shift in my attitude and my interpretive comments. During such regressive states, my interpretations focused less on typical borderline mechanisms and part object transferences, and more on the patient's conflicting needs to differentiate herself from me and for perfect understanding and caretaking. In short, differentiation conflicts seemed temporarily to predominate over pathological rapprochement conflicts.

I hope this case also illustrates my conviction that an ego-psychological object relations approach, integrated within an overall structural model of the mind and a developmental approach to structure formation, can be elaborated harmoniously into a contemporary psychoanalytic theory of psychotherapeutic technique.

REFERENCES

BALINT, M. (1968). *The Basic Fault: Therapeutic Aspects of Regression.* Great Britain: Tavistock Publications.

BERGERET, J. (1970). *Les Etats Limites. Revue Francaise de Psychoanalyse.* 34:605-633.

BIBRING, E. (1954). Psychoanalysis and the dynamic psychotherapies. *Journal of the American Psychoanalytic Association,* 2:745-770.

BION, W. R. (1965). *Transformations.* London: Heinemann.

BION, W. R. (1967). *Second Thoughts.* London: Heinemann.

BION, W. R. (1970). *Attention and Interpretation.* London: Tavistock.

BION, W. R. (1974). *Bion's Brazilian Lectures:1, Sao Paulo, 1973.* Ed. J. Salomao. Rio de Janeiro: Imago Editora Ltd.

BION, W. R. (1975). *Bion's Brazilian Lectures: 2, Rio/Sao Paulo, 1974.* Ed. J. Salomao. Rio de Janeiro: Imago Editora Ltd.

BION, W. R. (1977). *Two Papers: The Grid and Caesura.* Ed. J. Salomao. Rio de Janeiro: Imago Editora Ltd.

FURER, M. (1977). Personality organization during the recovery of a severely disturbed young child. In *Borderline Personality Disorders,* ed. P. Hartocollis. New York: International Universities Press, pp. 457-473.

GILL, M. M. (1954). Psychoanalysis and exploratory psychotherapy. *Journal of the American Psychoanalytic Association,* 2:771-797.

GIOVACCHINI, P. (1975). *Psychoanalysis of Character Disorders.* New York: Jason Aronson.

GREEN, A. (1977). The borderline concept. In *Borderline Personality Disorders,* ed. P. Hartocollis. New York: International Universities Press, pp. 15-44.

GRINKER, R. R. (1975). Neurosis, psychosis, and the borderline states. In *Comprehensive Textbook of Psychiatry—II,* ed. by Freedman, Sadock and Kaplan. Baltimore: Williams & Wilkins, pp. 845-850.

HARTOCOLLIS, P. (1977). Affects in borderline disorders. In *Borderline Personality Disorders, ed. P. Hartocollis.* New York: International Universities Press, pp. 495-507.

JACOBSON, E. (1954). Contribution to the metapsychology of psychotic identifications. *Journal of the American Psychoanalytic Association*, 2:239-262.

KERNBERG, O. et al. (1972). Psychotherapy and psychoanalysis. Final report of the Menninger Foundation's Psychotherapy Research Report. *Bulletin of the Menninger Clinic.* Topeka, Kansas. Vol. 36, Nos. 1/2. January-March.

KERNBERG, O. (1975). *Borderline Conditions and Pathological Narcissism.* New York: Jason Aronson.

KERNBERG, O. (1976a). *Object-Relations Theory and Clinical Psychoanalysis.* New York: Jason Aronson.

KERNBERG, O. (1976b). Technical considerations in the treatment of borderline personality organization. *Journal of the American Psychoanalytic Association,* 24:795-829.

LITTLE, M. (1957). "R"—The analyst's total response to his patient's needs. *International Journal of Psycho-Analysis,* 38:240-254.

LITTLE, M. (1960). On basic unity. *International Journal of Psycho-Analysis,* 41:377-384.

LITTLE, M. (1966). Transference in borderline states. *International Journal of Psycho-Analysis,* 47:476-485.

MAHLER, M. (1968). *On Human Symbiosis and the Vicissitudes of Individuation, Infantile Psychosis.* New York: International Universities Press.

MAHLER, M. (1971). A study of separation-individuation process and its possible application to borderline phenomena in the psychoanalytic situation. *Psychoanalytic Study of the Child,* 26:403-424.

MAHLER, M. (1972). On the first three subphases of separation-individuation process. *International Journal of Psycho-Analysis,* 53:333-338.

MAHLER, M. and KAPLAN, L. (1977). Developmental aspects in the assessment of narcissistic and so-called borderline personalities. In *Borderline Personality Disorders,* ed. P. Hartocollis. New York: International Universities Press, pp. 71-85.

MASTERSON, J. (1972). *Treatment of the Borderline Adolescent: A Developmental Approach.* New York: Wiley-Interscience.

MASTERSON, J. (1976). *Psychotherapy of the Borderline Adult: A Developmental Approach.* New York: Brunner/Mazel.

NELSON, M. (1967). Effect of paradigmatic techniques on the psychic economy of borderline patients. In *Active Psychotherapy,* ed. H. Greenwald. New York: Atherton Press, pp. 63-89.

RINSLEY, D. (1977). An object-relations view of borderline personality. In *Borderline Personality Disorders,* ed. P. Hartocollis. New York: International Universities Press, pp. 47-70.

SEARLES, H. (1965). *Collected Papers on Schizophrenia and Related Subjects.* New York: International Universities Press.

SEARLES, H. (1977). Dual- and multi-identity processes in borderline ego functioning. In *Borderline Personality Disorders*, ed. P. Hartocollis. New York: International Universities Press, pp. 441-455.

VOLKAN, V. (1975). *Clinical Correlates of Primitive Internalized Object Relations*. International Universities Press, pp. xiii-xvii.

WINNICOTT, D. W. (1958). *Collected Papers: Through Paediatrics to Psycho-Analysis*. New York: Basic Books.

WINNICOTT, D. W. (1960). Ego distortion in terms of true and false self. In *The Maturational Process and the Facilitating Environment*. New York: International Universities Press, 1965. Chapter 12:140-152.

WINNICOTT, D. W. (1965). *The Maturational Process and the Facilitating Environment*. New York: International Universities Press.

WOLBERG, A. R. (1973). *The Borderline Patient*. New York: Intercontinental Medical Book Corp.

ZETZEL, E. R. (1971). A developmental approach to the borderline patient. *American Journal of Psychiatry*, 127:867-871.

Discussion

Dr. Masterson: I feel at a great disadvantage today in discussing Dr. Kernberg's paper and let me tell you why. As anyone who has read anything that I have written on the borderline knows, I have been a keen student of Dr. Kernberg's work. From his point of view that could be for better or for worse. Let me tell you how I learn from him. When I first read a paper of his, I reel back sort of overwhelmed, confused and a little angry at him for making me work so hard. Then I carry it around for a number of weeks, going over it paragraph by paragraph until I finally get what it is he is trying to tell me—what new devilishly complex, multiply determined, paradoxically appearing phenomenon he is revealing to my gaze. Once I've reached this stage, his paper seems to fit together so clearly and completely and, in truth, has so opened my eyes that I wonder what all the trouble was in the first place.

My disadvantage today is that I'm still in that first stage, since I just received the paper yesterday and have only had a chance to read it once. Nevertheless, I shall try to harness my confusion to make a few confused remarks. There is so much with which I agree that I can mainly emphasize a few of the points. I think he outlines again beautifully and well, as he has elsewhere, the specific, technical ways in which classical psychoanalytic theory of symptom formation as a compromise between instinct and defense has not been very helpful with borderline patients—and why an integrated object relations ego psychological approach is necessary. I agree with his emphasis that primitive transferences, which are immediate and available, predominate as resistances and must be focused upon immediately. His view that classical psychoanalytic theory applies best to patients with good ego strength reminds me of a story. Ruth Easser, M.D., from Columbia University gave a paper in which she described the criteria for a good analytic patient. The analyst who discussed her paper was Director of Training at Downstate Psychiatric Institute. He had applied her criteria to one hundred candidates for the psychoanalytic school and not a single one qualified.

I also agree with his notion that the therapist maintain a position of technical neutrality, that the techniques are clarification, which I often call confrontation, and interpretation, and that manipulation should be avoided; however, some deviation has to occur in order to keep the patient alive sometimes, as well as to keep the patient functioning, and the therapist must learn to integrate the cognitive as well as the emotional aspects of his understanding of the work. It seems to me that each one of our speakers today is an excellent illustration of that fact.

There is a great deal of argument currently over whether a given treatment is or is not analysis. It seems to me Dr.

Kernberg's approach, viewing it as a spectrum of psycho-analytic psychotherapies and psychoanalysis, is more faithful to the clinical material and of more use.

Dr. Giovacchini: I'm with the audience at this moment because I never read the paper. I don't know whether what I have to say is an agreement or disagreement. This is not unlike the way I feel with borderline patients.

I made the point at the 1965 meetings of the American Psychoanalytic Association that the treatment of choice for borderline patients was psychoanalysis, and I was vehemently attacked. I have the feeling that Kernberg made the same point today. I always believed that the more severe the case, the more one had to adhere to the psychoanalytic model; with the less severe, one could afford to wander away from it. Of course, there are special conditions and limitations. Just because a patient is sick, he is not necessarily a good candidate for analysis. But he often is and I think Kernberg was speaking to that point in one section of his paper. This can also be supported theoretically. For these very sensitive patients, for these very fragile egos, any kind of manipulation, any kind of attempt to run their life becomes an assault. I call it an intrusion. The patient views it as an attack. True, in some instances the therapist may think he's gratifying basic infantile needs and this may lead to some degree of comfort in the therapeutic relationship, but it can also lead to a suicide. Attempts at gratification do not really meet basic needs. Mother's milk to an adult will not be nourishing. If one tries to furnish it, it can lead to unmanageable frustration. At best, it may create a mutual delusion, a kind of megalomanic collusion between patient and therapist, that does not result in resolution and progress.

I have to consider classification, because everyone has referred to it in discussing my paper. I wanted to avoid the topic, but I see that I can't, so, reluctantly, I have to return to the subject of diagnosis. We have to acknowledge, at the very beginning, that we don't really know what we are talking about when we speak of borderline. Kernberg has one definition; I have another. What makes his definition better than mine? It's quite arbitrary. We may have our reasons for constructing these particular diagnostic labels, but these have not been spelled out at this moment. I feel that every patient who has a character defect, in contrast to a psychoneurotic patients (and I wonder if they even exist), is borderline. These patients are often hovering on the edge of a psychosis and, in this phenomenological sense, they are borderline. I believe the spectrum from early schizoid states to the patients Searles has been talking about up to the more structured patients Kernberg and Masterson are discussing can be considered borderline from the phenomenological viewpoint. This is not a closed topic. It's something that deserves a lot of examination, and I don't think we are going to resolve this issue. It's going to take years before we come to some kind of consensus. It's enough that we know that we are talking about similar kinds of patients and not have to worry at this moment about the labels. I think that's much too premature.

My criticism of Kernberg is—well, first, I'll say something positive as has been our custom. He is quite right in wanting to construct an ego-psychological object relation model. On the negative side, he has not gone far enough with it. What he has failed to do is to give up, as sufficiently as he should, previous models. He still retains much of the classical model. He retains much of Hartman's energic hypotheses (1939). He retains much of drive theory. He retains much of Klein (1950). There are many good things in these particular models but he has not synthesized them. He gives the illusion of systemization and organization but, in fact, he has taken large segments of these models and additively combined them. Clinically, this is not helpful.

Finally, I would like to ask Dr. Kernberg why he considers his therapy with the patient he presented psychoanalytic psychotherapy. He has not shown how it differs from psychoanalysis.

———————

Dr. Searles: I have a certain kind of conscientiousness that led me to send my paper to Dr. Masterson a few days before the deadline, a month ago, and I received Dr. Kernberg's paper at 10 p.m. last evening. It does hamper one in giving to the paper such a degree of thought as this paper warrants. I have admired Dr. Kernberg's writings for a considerable number of years now and regard him as a very brilliant theoretician and, undoubtedly, clinician also. I find each of his papers complex, difficult for me to grasp, but eminently worthy of careful study. When he says that "psychoanalytic therapy does not attempt as its goal the full resolution of unconscious conflicts and therefore of resistances but rather a partial resolution of some" and so on, it seems to me that he tends to maintain the illusion, certainly in many people's minds, that real psychoanalysis, if carried through to successful completion, resolves all of the patient's unconscious conflicts, and to me that is nonsense. Our lives are always filled with unconscious conflict. A successful psychoanalysis in the strict sense of the word would, in my mind, help the patient to gain really maximal access to his unconscious conflicts, but not to resolve all of them. And the trouble with this kind of phraseology is that it comes close to implying something which I, of course, know Dr. Kernberg does not intend to imply—namely, it tends to imply that the patient becomes very largely free from an unconscious, which I am confident Dr. Kernberg does not at all mean to imply. But it all tends to feed into a very regrettable picture of a well analyzed analyst as one who is literally free from unconscious conflicts in himself. So that he is facing a patient who is, as I was saying earlier, regarded as containing all of the psychopathology in the consulting room. Similarly, he later on speaks of expressive psychotherapy, wherein a systematic analysis of all transference paradigms, or a systematic resolution of transference neurosis by interpretation alone, is definitely not attempted. Here, again, it's implied that in psychoanalysis as strictly defined all transference paradigms are resolved. I cannot accept that. I think that it is important that we do not accept what are, in my opinion, illusions.

A bit later he is saying that "these object relations determine the characteristics of primitive transference, that is, of highly fantastic unreal precipitates of early object relations that do not reflect directly the real object relations of infancy and childhood" and so on. I would take issue here with the phrase "highly fantastic" and the word "unreal." Family therapy with schizophrenic patients and their families is one of the settings where one can get an appreciation of how genuinely remarkably disordered the childhood environment of these persons was. So that I want to suggest to you that in this passage Dr. Kernberg is going too far in calling these unreal percipitates. Again, I think we do the patient a disservice if we fail to discern and ascertain that there is some actual reality in his reactions—distorted, to be sure, but not unreal. They are not that far off base, given the nature of their childhood environments.

A bit later on in the paper, in terms of the treatment approach he is recommending—which makes eminently good sense to me, I will say at the outset, in very large part excellent sense—he speaks about the importance of starting out from the interpretation of the here and now only, and then leading into genetic reconstruction at later stages of the treatment. Again, I don't quarrel with that, but would suggest that this very focus on the here and now should also include attention to the real contributions that the analyst is making to the disturbed state of the here and now. I want to remind you of a paper of mine that I mentioned this morning, a 1972 paper, "The Role of the Delusional Transference of the Patient's Realistic Perceptions of the Analyst"—that is, the real way in which I was contributing to the patient's delusional experiences. It's comparable with what I suggested a few minutes ago about the reality of the disturbed environment in the patient's childhood.

Here I want to mention briefly a book, the reading of which I'm just completing now; it's called *The Bipersonal Field* by Robert Langs. Langs' book is, I think, fascinating and important in a number of regards—important because it presents in a detailed, well documented way the unconscious contributions that the therapist (in that instance the book is based on his teaching of residents) makes to the tangled and difficult transference reactions that the patient gets into. I think one gets the sense all the way through that this kind of thing happens in the hands of the most experienced and best analyzed of analysts. It's the kind of thing that is very much neglected in the literature and I recommend the book very highly to you.

I strongly concur with many, many things in Dr. Kernberg's paper, and one of them is his saying, "It is very important for the therapist working with borderline patients to be able to integrate both cognitive and emotional aspects in his understanding of the therapeutic situation, and the idealization of either the cognitive ('containing') or the emotional ('holding'), as opposed to each other, seriously limits a psychoanalytic psychotherapeutic approach with borderline cases." I found in recent years that I was starting, I thought, to very much idealize some state of things that I think does exist in clinical experience that I was calling preambivalent symbiosis as part of the therapeutically symbiotic phase. I think it does exist. It is to be found. But I came to realize that I was idealizing it in a fashion.

At this point I want to suggest that it is a testimony to the versatility of borderline patients that they are able to utilize the analytic abilities of analysts of quite different personality types. And I think you see a certain range among the four here. There are certain of us inclined much more toward the diagnostic orientation and others of us inclined more toward, what I call anyway the kind of symbiotic interaction with the patient.

I was thinking at one point in Dr. Kernberg's paper that

whether or not his concepts have rather direct value at that particular juncture to his patient, they have an eminently necessary and worthy function in Dr. Kernberg's own state of well-being in the work. I think we need to work out some style, stylistic approach and, hopefully, some body of theoretical concepts that make sense to oneself so that one can work in a way that one finds meaningful to oneself. I think that the one thing that put me off from the paper was a kind of note that if I'm going to be right about this I have to agree with Dr. Kernberg, and I cannot do so all across the board. I admire his brilliance and in many places I strongly agree with him; but he must allow us all room enough to develop our own particular individual set of approaches.

Dr. Kernberg: Regarding Dr. Masterson's comments, I think he implied, somewhat humorously, "Who knows whether there is any patient with good ego strength at all?" I believe that there are many patients for whom a standard psychoanalytic approach can be used without modifications of parameters of technique, and where I could see myself working quite similarly to many colleagues in psychoanalysis who don't use object relations concepts except at a rather theoretical level. But, with borderline patients I find it very difficult to do psychoanalytic psychotherapy without using object relations concepts at the clinical level.

Dr. Masterson did not pick up something I thought he might interpret as a criticism of his approach, namely, my strong criticism of supportive psychotherapy. It seems to me that Dr. Masterson's suggestion that psychoanalytic psychotherapy with borderline patients starts out with supportive psychotherapy and then becomes interpretive is only apparently different from my approach: If I read correctly what Dr. Masterson means by "supportive," he thinks of very active structuralization of the treatment situation and of confronting the patient with his primitive defensive operations, which I see as in harmony with an analytic approach.

Regarding Dr. Giovacchini's comments, I know Dr. Giovacchini has all along been on the side of those who attempted to treat these patients with non-modified psychoanalysis. He has contributed to the increasing conviction among psychotherapists that a psychoanalytic approach or analytic psychotherapy can be used with these patients. I think that, nowadays, supportive psychotherapy for borderline patients is rightly being abandoned in the relevant literature, although it is still quite prevalent in day-to-day experience.

I don't share Dr. Giovacchini's pessimism about the possibility of making a diagnosis of borderline conditions. I think that clinically it can be made in ways that can be documented, and I am part of a research group that is attempting to contribute to clarifying this issue. From a clinical viewpoint, the combination of the presence of identity diffusion, predominance of primitive defensive operations, and maintenance of reality testing defines borderline conditions. On the other hand, in neurotic illness and less severe character pathology there is identity integration, predominance of repression and related mechanisms, and consolidation of the tripartite intrapsychic structure. In contrast to both neurotic and borderline pathology, in schizophrenic and other psychotic illness reality testing is lost. I have proposed elsewhere that reality testing as well as identity diffusion can be defined operationally and tested clinically. I think there are behavioral manifestations of these structural characteristics that can be evaluated clinically. This is an area that I think will be clarified further through research now in progress.

It is true that I retain much of the classical model of psychoanalysis. I have been puzzled by the insistent attempts in the psychoanalytic literature to oppose a structural approach to object relations theory approaches: I see them as various aspects within the same theoretical framework.

To the question, how did what I did with this patient differ from psychoanalysis proper? I would answer: First of all, I tried to interpret resistances systematically—in this respect the case was like psychoanalysis. Second, I focused predominantly upon the transference, and again, in this way treated this case as in psychoanalysis. However, interpretation of the transference was not systematic, and there were long periods of time in which the patient's incapacity to be fully aware of the immediate reality of the therapeutic situation and her almost delusional attitudes toward me required the clarification of that reality. This means that, for practical purposes, the clarification of reality and clarification of the patient's interpretation of my comments took precedence over transference interpretation as such. In other words, for extended times, clarification and confrontation were predominant tools, with very little interpretation. In addition, there was a deviation from technical neutrality, because this patient had severe suicidal tendencies, and there was a need to protect her life that required, temporarily, a team approach to the treatment. A specialized nurse saw the patient for several months, and the distortion of technical neutrality derived from this team approach required, in turn, repeated focusing on the interpretation of this distortion of the therapeutic situation; all of this, I think, stretches the concept of psychoanalysis rather far. I hope this illustrates why I am saying that, tactically, looking at this case session by session, it sounds like psychoanalysis, but if you look at it over a long period of time—strategically—you can see the difference. And I think there is an advantage to keeping this difference, because it helps to clarify techniques and the boundaries between different approaches.

Regarding Dr. Searles' comments, I agree with his criticism that the definition of psychoanalysis as a full or total resolution of unconscious conflicts is rather presumptuous. I agree that there is no such thing as a "full" resolution of transference neurosis, and that all of us continue having unconscious conflicts and unresolved problems which are potentially dangerous sources of blind spots, but also may indirectly provide empathy with the more primitive conflicts of emotional life from which our patients suffer. I think that, in this connection, I hope you have also become aware of how close in many ways Dr. Searles' and my attitudes are regarding the interpretation of transference. I have found that, although the parents and the family situation of borderline patients have been extremely disturbed, very often they were so in different ways from what the patient tells us. So there are patient mythologies—his history as perceived chaos, the relation of which to the real chaos that existed in the family is indirect.

Dr. Searles stresses that, when we discuss the here and now interaction, we also have to accept the contribution made to it by the therapist himself. I agree with that, and it seems to me that, if a therapist of the borderline patient is always nice and friendly and is never affected by the transference, he is not really with it. We all have periods in which we are angry and upset, bored, struggle against falling sleep, and so on. My point is that these emotional reactions have to be analyzed by the therapist privately, in terms of where they come from, their components, to what extent the patient is inducing such reaction in us, and to what extent our own conflicts are being activated. I think there are dangers on both extremes: If, on the one hand, we say all of this comes from the patient, this fosters a denial of the countertransference, which feeds into the patient's psychopathology and makes us the "perfect human beings" with whom the patient can never really identify. If, on the other hand, we see in every disappointment of the patient our own fault, I think we fall into the danger of letting ourselves be controlled by the patient's aggressive omnipotent control, or of seducing the patient into the assumption that his symptoms are a result of our imperfections. This leads to perpetuating an unrealistic treatment atmosphere in which the patient can thrive as long as he feels he lives in an unreal, perfect world. So, it is important to analyze our own contributions without becoming guilt-ridden about them, without letting the patient's aggression enter into our superego.

In this connection, I think Langs' basic theoretical conception involves the same problem. He suggests analyzing the "bipersonal field" as though it were an almost symmetrical pathology of patient and therapist. I think that is a problem in treating very sick patients: To be in touch with them, one has to establish contact with primitive aspects in oneself, but that is very different from thinking that there is, therefore, no difference in the pathology of patient and therapist.

There has to be room for different styles of treatment,

and I hope that we can preserve this difference. I think the important thing is that we try to develop an integrative theoretical frame that permits us to translate from one personal style to another, and to clarify the general systems properties of the treatment. To say that therapy is an art rather than a science can result in a kind of mystical, antiscientific approach, which has happened to certain therapists who have felt that it is mostly the quality of the personality of the therapist that is important, and this feeds into the need for primitive idealization of borderline patients. There has to be balance between a personal style of therapy and an objective, stable frame of reference, that is, a theory of psychopathology and a theory of technique that bind our style and permit scientific research.

Dr. Masterson: Dr. Giovacchini feels that the borderline cannot be defined Dr. Kernberg feels that it can be defined. There seems to be quite a conflict here. I suppose it's clear that I share Dr. Kernberg's view. It brings to mind a story. There was a man who worked for many years with Mahler and her work here in New York and then he took a year's sabbatical and he went to London to work with Bowlby. And those of you who are familiar with Bowlby's work know that it's more or less in the same area as Mahler's. So this man who had worked with Mahler began talking to Bowlby about Mahler's work and he said, "Well, why don't you give me something that she has written and let me read it." So he gave him some of Mahler's papers. The next morning Bowlby came down and said, "Somebody's going to have to translate this for me. It gives me a terrible headache to read it."

Dr. Giovacchini: The borderline patient is frequently misunderstood and I'm being misunderstood. I didn't say the borderline state can't be defined. I think it can be defined. I just simply say it has not been adequately defined and that we're not in a position at this moment to accept anyone's arbitrary definition.

REFERENCES

HARTMAN, H. (1939). *Ego Psychology and the Problem of Adaptation*. New York: International Universities Press.

KLEIN, M. (1950). *Contributions to Psychoanalysis*. London: Hogarth Press.

LANGS, ROBERT (1976). *The Bipersonal Field*. New York: Jason Aronson.

SEARLES, H. F. (1972). The function of the patient's realistic perceptions of the analyst in delusional transference. *Brit. J. Med. Psychol.*, 45:1-18.

Chapter 4

The Borderline Adult:

Transference Acting-out

and Working-through

James F. Masterson, M.D.

INTRODUCTION

The critical question that dominated early research (Frosch, 1964, 1967; Knight, 1954a, b; Schmideberg, 1947; Stern, 1938, 1945; Zetzel, 1971) on the borderline syndrome —should the patient have supportive or analytic psychotherapy—seems to have been resolved in recent years with the general acceptance of the notion that many borderline patients do have the capacity to work through their conflicts in intensive psychoanalytic psychotherapy (Giovacchini, 1975; Heinmann, 1955; Kernberg, 1968, 1975; Knight, 1954a, b; Little, 1951; Mahler, 1968, 1975; Masterson, 1972, 1975, 1976, 1977, 1978; Masterson & Rinsley, 1975; Rinsley, 1974, 1977; Rosenfeld, 1958; Searles, 1967, 1969, 1977).

The next question that has come to occupy the center stage concerns what therapeutic techniques are necessary to achieve this objective. Some authors urged classical psychoanalysis (Giovacchini, 1975; Heinmann, 1955; Klein, 1952; Segal, 1964; Winnicott, 1965), others opposed it, warning that it led to prolonged rage-filled episodes of transference psychosis, which produced a therapeutic stalemate (Friedman, 1975).

This question about therapeutic technique has been increasingly and vividly brought home to me by numerous consultations requested to evaluate the lack of progress of patients in psychoanalytic psychotherapy with other therapists. These requests came from adolescents and their parents, from adults —some of whom were therapists themselves, and occasionally from the therapist doing the treatment. Sometimes, patient and therapist mutually requested a consultation. A few examples will illustrate:

A 17-year-old boy had been in treatment for two and a half years, twice a week, for complaints of depression, rage outbursts and severe compulsions that had caused him to drop out of school. Although he got along well with his therapist and his rage outbursts had decreased, he remained depressed and compulsive and was still not back in school. Two interviews, which involved my confronting his efforts to manipulate me to ask questions, rather than his telling his own story, triggered a rage outburst that then led to his awareness that he had similarly manipulated his therapist into directing the interviews with questions, thereby reinforcing the transference acting-out of his dependency needs.

A young man, age 21, with severe depression, passivity and inhibitions since the age of 15, that had led to much drug ingestion, managed to drag himself through college with psychotherapy ranging from one to three times a week. He then collapsed after graduation. He draped himself over the chair like a wet dish rag, remained silent and waited. My bringing this behavior to his attention triggered a response similar to that of the previously described patient. He felt I bore the entire responsibility for the interview.

A young woman, age 18, with a four-year history of anorexia nervosa had had one year of psychotherapy, three times a week on the couch. Her analyst said little, and what little affect she had originally shown dried up. After a year of a compliant pretense at therapy, she discontinued.

A woman therapist in her mid-thirties, after 13 years of analytic psychotherapy four times a week, had a brief psychotic episode precipitated by a separation experience. This frightened her and caused her to question the strength of her character structure, as well as the effectiveness of her long course of treatment.

Two other women therapists, also in their thirties, had been in analytic psychotherapy for five years, four times a week, and felt they were "stuck" in the working-through phase, which, indeed, they were.

At first glance, one might suspect that some of these were difficult or actually untreatable patients, or that the therapists either lacked adequate knowledge about therapy or had such severe personal problems or such a countertransference that they were unable to conduct the treatment. Although this was occasionally the case, the most common problem with the treatment of almost all of these cases was that the therapist did not understand the psychodynamics and clinical manifestations of the patients' transference acting-out and therefore could not manage it therapeutically.

This paper describes how the intrapsychic structure of the borderline personality (split object relations unit, split ego) evolves from the separation-individuation failure and later becomes manifest in psychotherapy in various forms of transference acting-out. It then explains why, and demonstrates how, the therapeutic techniques of confrontation and interpretation deal with the acting-out and provide the necessary framework to allow the patient to work through his conflicts. This point of view about psychotherapy of the borderline is shared by a number of other authors, each of whom, however, comes to his conclusions from a slightly different theoretical perspective (Adler, 1973; Adler & Myerson, 1975; Eisler, 1953; Frosch, 1964, 1967; Kernberg, 1968, 1975; Rinsley, 1974, 1977).

FREUD ON TRANSFERENCE ACTING-OUT AND WORKING-THROUGH

It is first necessary to briefly review the essentials of the relationship between transference acting-out and working-through which were so clearly described by Freud (1915). To adapt this brilliant discussion to the borderline patient we have only to substitute the words transference acting-out for the phrase "expressing what is forgotten in behavior," splitting for regression and confrontation for interpretation. Freud highlighted the following: The patient remembers nothing, but expresses it in action. He reproduces it not in his memory but in his behavior. He repeats it in his transference acting-out.

The compulsion to repeat an action which replaces the impulse to remember is activated in treatment through the transference relationship. The repetition compulsion to act is curbed and turned into a motive for remembering by the handling of the transference (in the borderline, confrontation of transference acting-out). The repetition compulsion then gets full play in the transference and in the interview via thoughts, feelings, fantasies and memories. Repetitive reactions in the transference evoke affects which, when not discharged by acting-out, lead to the awakening of memories. This sets the stage for working-through.

One must allow the patient time to get to know the resistance of which he is ignorant, to work it through, to overcome it. Only by living the resistances through in this way will the patient be conscious of their existence and power. It is an arduous task for the patient and a trial of patience for the therapist. Theoretically one may correlate the working through with the "abreaction" of quantities of affect pent up by repression found in hypnosis.

THE BORDERLINE TRANSFERENCE: A DEVELOPMENTAL PERSPECTIVE

The borderline transference consists of the activation and alternate projection upon the therapist of the patient's primitive, split, positive and negative object relations part-units, which are then acted out in the transference. The origins of the split object relations unit, its functions in the patient's intrapsychic life, its relationship with the therapeutic alliance, its manifestations in transference, as well as the therapeutic use of confrontation to manage it, are best understood if approached from a developmental perspective (Masterson & Rinsley, 1975; Masterson, 1976).

From a developmental perspective the intrapsychic structure consists of the split object relations unit and the split ego.

Split Object Relations Unit

The mother of the future borderline patient rewards the child for regressive clinging but withdraws her libidinal availability at the child's efforts towards separation-individuation. This crisis occurs probably during the rapproachement sub-phase of separation-individuation when this withdrawal produces a developmental arrest characterized by a fixation of the ego, along with an abandonment depression. These have been described in detail elsewhere (Masterson, 1972, 1976; Masterson & Rinsley, 1975).

These two interactions with the mother—i.e., reward for regression, withdrawal for separation-individuation—are introjected by the child, along with their associated part-object and part-self representations, to form the essential intrapsychic structure of the borderline—the split object relations unit. These two part-units, illustrated in Table 1, each consisting of a part-object representation, a part-self representation, together with the affect that links them, can be called the rewarding and the withdrawing part-units; the former is primarily cathected with libidinal energy and the withdrawing unit with aggressive energy. They are kept separated from each other by the splitting defense mechanism.

Split Ego

A substantial part of the borderline's ego fails to undergo the expected transformation from the pleasure principle to the reality principle, resulting in a split ego, part of which is motivated by the pleasure principle and part by the reality principle. The former can be termed the pathologic ego, while the latter can be called the reality ego. Why does this pathologic pleasure ego persist? As the child's self representation begins to differentiate from the object representation of the mother, i.e., as the child begins to separate, he now experiences the abandonment depression at the threat of loss

TABLE 1

Split Object Relations Unit of Borderline

REWARDING PART UNIT*	WITHDRAWING PART UNIT*
Part-Object Representations	*Part-Object Representations*
A maternal part-object which offers approval, support and supplies for regressive and clinging behavior.	A maternal part-object which is attacking, critical, hostile, angry, withdrawing supplies and approval in the face of assertiveness or other efforts toward separation-individuation.
Affect	*Affect—Abandonment Depression*
Feeling good, gratification of the wish for reunion, being taken care of, receiving unconditional love.	Suicidal depression, homicidal rage, panic, helplessness and hopelessness, emptiness and void—feelings of loss of vital supplies.
Part-Self Representation	*Part-Self Representation*
A conscious part-self representation of being the good, passive, compliant child. A split object part-self representation of being grandiose, unique, special and able to control the mother and hence the environment, i.e., to coerce the environment into actions that would resonate with and activate the rewarding object relations unit (RORU).	A part-self representation of being inadequate, bad, helpless, guilty, empty, etc.

* RORU—Rewarding Object Relations Part Unit
  WORU—Withdrawing Object Relations Part Unit

or withdrawal of supplies; at the same time, the mother continues to encourage and to reward those aspects of her child's behavior—passivity and regressiveness—which enable her to continue to cling to him.

Thus, the mother encourages and rewards in the child the pathological ego's key defense mechanisms of avoidance of individuation and denial of the reality of separation, which in turn allows the persistence of the fantasied wish for reunion, which is then reinforced as a defense against the abandonment depression. Thus part of the ego fails to undergo the necessary transformation from reliance upon the pleasure principle to reliance upon the reality principle, for to do so would mean acceptance of the reality of separation, which would bring on the abandonment depression.

RELATIONSHIP BETWEEN SPLIT OBJECT RELATIONS UNIT AND SPLIT EGO

The mother's rewarding and withdrawing responses encourage the development of an alliance between the child's rewarding part-unit and his pathological (pleasure) ego, the primary purpose of which is to promote the "good" feeling and to defend against the feeling of abandonment associated with the withdrawing part-unit. The patient experiences this part-unit as ego-syntonic, i.e., it enables him to feel good. The regressive, destructive behavior itself is denied.

The withdrawing part-unit (part-self representation, part-object representation and feelings of abandonment) becomes activated by actual experiences of separation (or of loss), or by life situations which require independence and individuation to cope, or by moves toward separation-individuation within the therapeutic process, all of which symbolize earlier life experiences which evoked the mother's withdrawal of supplies.

The alliance between the rewarding part-unit and the pathological (pleasure) ego is in turn activated by the resurgence of the withdrawing part-unit. The purpose of this operation is defensive, to restore the wish for reunion, thereby relieving the feeling of abandonment. The rewarding part-unit thus becomes the borderline's principal defense against the painful affective state associated with the withdrawing part-unit. In terms of reality, however, both part-units are pathological: it is as if the patient has but two alternatives, i.e., either to feel bad and abandoned (withdrawing part-unit) or to feel good (rewarding part-unit), at the cost of denial of reality and self destructive behavior. The borderline patient early becomes accustomed to and identifies as his own a life-style based on the sacrifice of adaptation, i.e., coping with reality—to defend against separation anxiety and abandonment depression—i.e., the false self (Winnicott, 1965).

THERAPEUTIC ALLIANCE AND TRANSFERENCE: A DEVELOPMENTAL PERSPECTIVE

The borderline transference consists of the alternate activation and projection upon the therapist of each of the split object relations part-units. During those periods in which the patient projects the withdrawing part-unit (with its part-object representation of the withdrawing mother) on to the therapist, he perceives therapy as necessarily leading to feelings of abandonment, denies the reality of therapeutic benefit and activates the rewarding part-unit as a defense. When projecting the rewarding part-unit (with its reunion fantasy) on to the therapist, the patient "feels good" but, under the sway of the pathological (pleasure) ego, is usually found to be acting in a regressive, self-destructive manner. Both, however, represent forms of transference acting-out—an instant replay—in which the therapist is treated not as a real object upon whom infantile feelings are displaced, but as if he actually were the infantile object. It is as if the therapist enters this already ongoing system and becomes the latest and most important target for the projection of each of the object relations part-units. The transference acting-out differs from a transference psychosis in that when the projection is brought to the patient's attention he is able to distinguish between his projected feelings and the reality of the therapist.

PSYCHOTHERAPY

In the initial stage of treatment a therapeutic alliance is gradually activated by confronting the destructive aspects of the patient's transference acting-out—either the distorted perceptions involved in the projection of the withdrawing unit on the therapist or the regressive destructive behavior associated with the rewarding unit projection.

The term confrontation is used not in the sense of the therapist taking his aggression out on the patient or challenging him, but rather, in the sense of bringing to the attention of the patient's observing ego the denied realistically destructive aspects of his defense mechanisms, i.e., splitting, projection, projective identification, clinging, avoidance, denial and acting-out. This stage can be stormy as the tenuous and fragile alliance is repeatedly shattered each time the WORU (Withdrawing Object Relations Unit) is activated.

Once the patient has developed an internalized object representation of the therapist, the therapeutic alliance becomes fully activated and now functions counter to the alliance between the patient's RORU and his pathological ego, battling with the latter for control of the patient's motivations and actions. As the therapeutic alliance gains the upper hand, the patient turns from his lifelong reliance on the RORU pathological ego alliance for relief of his separation anxiety and abandonment depression to working-through in the transference.

Entrance into the working-through phase is signalled clinically by: fewer and fewer interruptions in the continuity of the therapeutic alliance as it takes over control of behavior from the RORU pathological ego alliance; a shift in the patient's perspective on the latter from being ego-syntonic to being ego-alien, symbolized by his assigning it a disparaging nickname such as creep, baby, monster, devil, etc.; more realistically constructive coping behavior so that daily life crises fade from the center of the therapeutic scene and the abandonment depression deepens and is linked to the emergence of early memories. Acting-out now becomes more localized in the transference where it must be again confronted, which again leads to more working-through. The result is a circular process of transference acting-out, confrontation, working-through, transference acting-out, confrontation, working-through with the debut of each new interaction in therapy. The resolution of one level of interaction through confrontation and working-through leads inevitably to more depression and then more defense—i.e., transference acting-out. The therapist must remain alert and not be lulled into a false sense of security by the transformation of one episode of transference acting-out into working-through, for as soon as that level of depression is worked through the next will again present itself as transference acting-out.

As the patient moves further into the working-through phase, the therapeutic alliance strengthens, as does the observing ego and reality perception. There is a corresponding deepening of awareness of the extraordinary ramifications of the WORU and it now becomes possible to deal with transference acting-out directly by interpretation. Before shifting to the interpretation the therapist must review each episode to be sure that the transference acting-out has not overwhelmed the patient's observing ego and reality perception.

CASE PRESENTATION: MANAGEMENT OF TRANSFERENCE ACTING-OUT

Peter, a 40-year-old man was referred by his cardiologist after repeated negative electrocardiograms, with complaints of episodes of severe attacks of chest pains, palpitations, grogginess, dizziness, nausea and sweating. Peter would panic each time the symptoms occurred and was convinced he was having a heart attack. He was in the process of divorcing his second wife after she had a severe depression for which she had to be hospitalized. Peter had felt abandoned and started an affair with another woman. He was ambivalent about a third marriage, feeling he couldn't afford a third divorce.

Past History

Peter was the oldest of three children, with a brother two years younger and a sister four years younger. He described his father as austere, forbidding, disapproving, stonefaced, successful and hardworking but never at home. The father was compulsively neat, rarely expressed anger or other emotion and considered Peter to be inadequate and a lightweight, while favoring his younger brother.

The mother was described as attractive, vivacious, and "used to be a lot of fun." Peter had been very close to her as a child and a young man. However, he felt that when the children grew up she had become depressed because she had nothing to do. Peter felt he was more like the mother than the father in that he liked a good time. He recalled resenting his brother, whose personality was more like the father's, since the time of the brother's birth when Peter was two.

His memories of his childhood were quite vague, but he did recall spending a good deal of time with the mother and the father's working from early morning until late at night. While he enjoyed himself with his mother, when father came home the house was filled with an atmosphere of doom and gloom.

He vividly recalled the terror experienced at having his tonsils out at age four. Ever since he had hated doctors. When he was examined by school doctors he used to get palpitations and be afraid of being sent back to the hospital.

He always got by in school, had an attractive, easygoing personality and made friends easily. He graduated college, married in his senior year and began to work for his father.

Intrapsychic Structure

Peter's rewarding object relations part-unit consisted of an omnipotent, all good mother image who provided supplies and "kept him safe and protected," as long as he remained dependent on her, fulfilling her needs to cling. Beneath this mother image was another mother image whose attentions and demands were engulfing.

Peter's affect was a global sense of feeling good and being loved, with a grandiose self representation of being unique and special through childish behavior.

The patient's WORU was much more complex and took more time to emerge. It consisted of an image of a mother who would not only abandon him, but who would annihilate him or leave him to die if he expressed himself or attempted to separate from her. This withdrawing object relations part-unit of the mother—encouraged by her behavior—was defended against by splitting it from the real mother and projecting it on to the father, whose part-image was that of a stern, cold, disapproving and punishing figure. The affect was one of intense rage and fear of abandonment which was equated with death and expressed in the somatic preoccupation with having a heart attack. The self-image was of a ghost without substance, an incompetent, a lightweight, of being inadequate, unmasculine, a creep.

The part-image of the engulfing mother, linked with feelings of panic at being devoured or swallowed up, only emerged much later.

Relationship with Oedipal Conflict

The intrapsychic structure was further complicated by the patient's having, in addition, another image of the father as a punitive, castrating oedipal rival for the mother. The splitting and projection of the WORU of the mother on the father and the image of the father as a punitive, castrating rival became fused through the mother's projections and father's behavior. The tonsillectomy experience at age four dramatized this fear. The patient's guilt about individuative strivings, combined with his guilt about oedipal strivings, led to his interpretation of the experience as an abandonment and a castration, thus condensing his separation anxiety and castration anxiety, i.e., condensing the preoedipal and the oedipal.

Defense Mechanisms of the Pathologic Ego

The defense mechanisms of the pathologic ego consisted primarily of massive splitting, avoidance of self-expression or efforts towards individuation, denial of the reality destructiveness of this behavior, projection and acting-out of the wish for reunion through clinging to mother and women.

Peter's suppression of self (thoughts, feelings and actions) was extreme. His actions were motivated either by the need to please or because he felt he "ought" to act in a specific way. Thoughts or feelings arising from within—i.e., that he *wanted* to act rather than felt he *should* act—produced great anxiety which was fantasized in the form of preoccupations with a heart attack and fear of dying.

The Therapeutic Task

The need or wish articulated in the fantasy which is concealed or hidden behind, but nonetheless motivates or drives, the RORU-pathologic ego alliance can be described by various synonyms: From an instinctual point of view it is an oral, dependent craving; from an object relations point of view it is gratification of the wish for reunion expressed by clinging to the object; from a descriptive point of view it is the wish to receive unconditional love, or to be taken care of.

Peter's transference acting-out consisted of efforts to manipulate me into actions which would resonate with and ostensibly gratify this fantasy and enable him to feel good, loved or special; or barring that, have me serve as a target upon which he could externalize and ventilate his lifelong rage at the frustrations of these wishes. From the psychopathological point of view it was seemingly a foolproof method. He couldn't lose—i.e., it enabled him to either feel loved and special or to relieve his tensions at the frustration of these wishes on the spot without having to face and accept their existence in his psyche. However, from the therapeutic point of view he couldn't win. The therapeutic task was to set reality limits to both these projections to enable him to become aware of their function in his intrapsychic life and thereby to lead him back to experiencing and working through his abandonment depression.

The Psychotherapy

Let us now examine the working-through phase of Peter's therapy which began after about 18 months during which he was seen four times a week. At one point, in the nineteenth month, Peter was still defending against awareness of his depression and the WORU by acting-out through clinging to his ex-wife. I confronted his clinging; I wondered why he was spending so much time with her, even having sexual intercourse, when his basic objective was to continue with the divorce. I pointed out that he was limiting her opportunities for other relationships, as well as his own, and making it difficult for both of them to resolve their feelings about the divorce. He replied, unwittingly revealing his fantasy: "I wish mother and everyone, even my ex-wife, would accept me as I am. I'm sure that mother still thinks I'm a child and will conform with her wishes. The rage is awful."

At this exact moment, when Peter took his first look at his wish for unconditional love from his mother and his rage at her failure to provide it, he completely blocked out feelings, sat silently and then suddenly turned and asked me to give him a match for his cigar. This raised an issue we fortunately had discussed a number of times—I did not carry matches and if he wanted to smoke in interviews he should bring his own. I refused to provide the matches, referring to our prior discussion, and inquired why he had asked for them. This query was met by more blocking and silence as the interview ended. However, he returned to the next interview with a full head of steam, in a rage at me for not giving him the match. I reminded him that we had several times discussed the need for him to bring his own matches if he wanted to smoke. When he agreed, I then went further and wondered if his rage could be related to the painful emotional content of the prior interview? Peter now turned from transference acting-out to working-through. He said, "I have been playing a game here with you about the matches." I now interpreted that he wished from me what he had wanted but felt he never received from his mother: unconditional acceptance. My not giving him the matches became a condition which triggered the re-enactment of the rage at his mother's conditions for love. However, instead of being a small, helpless, humiliated, dependent child, he was now—in the transference acting-out —strong and angry, and wanted to hit me and walk out.

I asked why he had never expressed that anger with his mother. He said, "I was afraid she'd leave me, abandon me. She loved my father and brother more than me."

The working-through continued into the next interview as Peter reported a dream that his mother had come into his room and had moved the nightstand around so that the two beds could be close together. In the dream he felt annoyed by her action.

Peter's free associations: "I held on to mother to avoid death and the infinity feeling. My lack of development was due to avoiding any feeling that wasn't good—i.e., based on her." At the same time he reported increasing depression with suicidal fantasies and a feeling state of being empty.

Peter then recalled a childhood memory of the feeling of dying at age eight. He was running to play basketball, got an anxiety attack and thought that he was going to die, panicked and ran back to his mother for reassurance. Mother told him that the soul lived on with those left behind. He thought, "What happens to me?" He continued working-through; "I was such a good kid and they didn't see it. All the good things in me (his individuation) were lost. They gave me no muscle to my character. If I'm successful in treatment I will die." If he gives up his clinging and individuates, he will die. This is a most common and ultimate fantasy of borderline patients that must be brought to awareness and worked through.

After Peter was well into the working-through process, he reported having recaptured—i.e., feeling and remembering —his earliest feelings of abandonment: "I feel this: Please don't hurt me, I'll be a good boy, don't reject me, don't throw me into infinity. I'm afraid I would panic and be helpless." The tonsils experience at age four reinforced these feelings and caused the first overt panic: "I knew something bad would happen. I wasn't told anything about it beforehand. The cloth was put over my face. My mother was squeezing my hand, then she left, the cloth remained. I saw this huge light surrounded by people with masks. I sat up and said,

'Please don't hurt me.' They held me down under anesthesia. I dreamed about the spiders. I woke up feeling lied to. How could she do that to me? She had the power."

Several months later, despite the intense and well sustained level of the working-through that Peter had attained, an interpretation triggered intense transference acting-out. In response to his associations, I interpreted to Peter that he had ceded his own power to effect change to his mother—i.e., she was omnipotent, he was helpless.

He was furious in the next interview: "I'm madder than hell at you. I can't be dependent on you. I'd like to walk out. You said there was too much of a child in me." I pointed out Peter's projection on me of his feelings of shame and inadequacy at his dependence on his mother and this led to further working-through. "I don't want to face the fact that mother didn't care for me and manipulated me. I see myself doing the same thing. If mother doesn't love me, who will? She was dependent on me to make her feel good. If I went along, nothing bad would happen to me; if I didn't go along, something bad could. She hated me, was nasty, vindictive, selfish. This is the point where I stop thinking and feeling."

Peter then reported a dream of his going back to the old game with the mother—a dream to defend against the affect emerging in the interviews. He questioned: "What is the huge investment in this game? It's safe, self expression is not." I now underlined that he played the game, the wish for reunion, to defend against fear, as if there were no other way to cope with it. This confrontation with his fear triggered more defensive transference acting-out. He was silent for awhile and then threw the ball back to me. He got angry when I didn't answer and said, "That's what I'm paying you for." After a long silence I interpreted that he was now trying to defend against his fear by acting-out the wish for reunion with me. This interpretation returned him to working-through. Peter replied: "I'm nothing without mother. I'm a vacuum. I'm afraid of not being, of evaporating. My existence is totally tied to mother. If I stayed inside what mother wanted, I was safe. If I stepped out, there was trouble. I gave mother total power."

Still later, Peter again acted out in the transference by asking me why I charged him when he missed an appointment. After I confronted him with our initial agreement on this issue, he ignored my remarks to express his anger about therapy as a one-way street, unjust, not giving him what he wanted.

In a still later interview he attempted transference acting-out by angrily saying that he knew he was not doing something right and demanding that I as the doctor did know and had to tell him what to do. When I asked why he felt so helpless, he exploded with his angry feeling that I was withholding. When I held the line he got depressed and responded: "I can't give myself any value. I give my parents' values more credence than my own." I then interpreted that he was externalizing on me his anger at their lack of support.

Near the end of treatment Peter was under great emotional pressure from the success of his individuation, was expressing his anger at the resulting frustration of the wish for unconditional love through fantasies and dreams rather than by transference acting-out, when suddenly without warning he said he wanted to cut down the number of weekly therapy sessions, which I interpreted as an effort to lessen the pressure for individuation, as well as to act out the anger in the transference for the frustration of the wish for unconditional love. He replied: "You're like my parents, saying I can't do it except four times a week, and I'm saying screw you, I'll show you and do it my way." I reiterated that he was externalizing and acting out in the transference his anger at his parents' emotional withdrawal for separation-individuation.

In the next interview he reported his feeling that he would rather fight me than face them. He did not want to admit they were bad because he felt they were so bad and it made him feel so depressed.

I will now end the case report as it has served its purpose of illustrating the dynamics and management of transference acting-out. Peter continued to a relatively successful conclusion of his therapy as I have reported elsewhere (Masterson, 1976). I saw him in follow-up two years after treatment stopped and his improvement has been maintained; beyond that he has continued to individuate.

DISCUSSION

These examples illustrate that the transference acting-out (the RORU pathologic ego alliance) is a defense against the underlying WORU part-unit with its abandonment depression and that confrontation of the former activates the latter. If the therapist confronts the transference acting-out of the RORU pathologic ego alliance (the resistance), that which it was a defense against—the abandonment depression—will emerge and the WORU will be projected on the therapist. As this is confronted, the patient will begin to work through the depression in the interviews and the experience will be assimilated by the observing ego. The results of the separation-individuation failure will be markedly attenuated or overcome as the patient's ego, freed of the need to defend against the abandonment depression, resumes its developmental path to autonomy.

Patient and therapist alike must learn to identify, endure, cope with and eventually resolve an apparent paradox: If the therapist does his job (confrontation) and the patient begins to respond (separate and individuate), the patient feels worse not better, i.e., more anger and depression. However, over time, as the resistances are resolved, these painful affects attenuate and give way to the patient's individuation process.

The onset of the working-through phase rekindles the patient's separation-individuation process and the therapist must be prepared in some instances for the emergence of acute symptoms, such as psychotic or suicidal episodes, feelings of depersonalization or unreality, or severe paranoid projections. These events are usually transient and respond to a fuller engagement of the transference and are not by themselves contraindications to maintaining the therapeutic momentum. The temporary use of drugs and/or various environmental arrangements to safeguard the patient are warranted at these times.

The clinical example illustrated the management of transference acting-out characterized by clinging in which the therapist must set limits to the patient's destructive actions. The management of the transference acting-out of the patient who uses distancing defenses, which I have described elsewhere, varies in that the therapist must set limits not so much to the patient's actions as to the patient's projections of feelings derived from the WORU on the therapist.

It should always be kept in mind that all patients cannot work through and therefore a thorough evaluation should be undertaken of each patient's potential for working-through.

Are the memories that are worked through memories of real events or fantasies based on feelings and distorted perceptions? In all probability they are both real events and patients' distorted elaborations of those events. It is important to keep in mind that the borderline patient is not dealing with a single memory or a traumatic event, but, rather, with an enduring pattern of interaction that not only has persisted throughout his entire lifetime, but has also been internalized and become part of his psyche.

In my experience the most therapeutic benefit is received if the patient can get to the bottom of what I call the tie that binds—the recognition that much of what underlies his pathologic behavior is his feeling that if he separates and individuates he and the mother will die. Parallel with this is the recognition of the hopelessness of the wish for unconditional love. This recognition is conveyed by a specific context of memories—which, however, focus on the meaning of events not so much in themselves but as seen within the matrix of the interaction. When these are faced in working-through, the burdensome anchor on the individuation process is lifted sufficiently for the patient's individuation to flower. Treatment is far from finished but the psychic balance has shifted sufficiently from the old emphasis on sacrificing adaptation to defense to a new emphasis on adaptation and coping with reality, coupled with the use of therapy to resolve the painful feeling states that result.

146   NEW PERSPECTIVES ON THE BORDERLINE ADULT

REFERENCES

ADLER, G. (1973). Hospital treatment of borderline patients. *Amer. J. Psych.,* 130:32-36.

ADLER, G. and MYERSON, P. (1973). *Confrontation in Psychotherapy.* New York: Science House.

BION, W. R. (1957). Differentiation of the psychotic from the non-psychotic personalities. *Int. J. Psycho-Anal.,* 38.

EISLER, K. (1953). The effects of the structure of the ego on psychoanalytic technique. *J. Amer. Psa. Assn.,* 1:104.

FREUD, S. (1915). Further recommendations in the technique of psychoanalysis, recollection, repetition and working through. *Collected Papers,* Vol. II. London: Hogarth Press, 1953, pp. 366-376.

FRIEDMAN, HENRY J. (1975). Psychotherapy of borderline patients: The influence of theory on technique. *Am. J. Psa.,* 132:101, Oct.

FROSCH, J. (1964). The psychotic character: Clinical psychiatric considerations. *J. Psych. Quart.,* 38:81-96.

FROSCH, J. (1967). Psychoanalytic considerations of the psychotic character. *J. Amer. Psa. Assn.,* 15:606-625.

GIOVACCHINI, P. (Ed.) (1975). *Psychoanalysis of Character Disorders.* New York: Jason Aronson.

HEINMANN, P. (1955). A combination of defense mechanisms in paranoid states. In *New Directions in Psycho-Analysis,* ed. Klein et al. London: Tavistock, and New York: Basic Books.

KERNBERG, O. (1968). The treatment of patients with borderline personality organization. *Int. J. Psa.,* 49:600-619.

KERNBERG, O. (1975). *Borderline Conditions and Pathological Narcissism.* New York: Science House, pp. 163-177.

KLEIN, M. (1952). The origins of transference. *Int. J. Psycho-Anal.,* 33.

KNIGHT, R. P. (1954). Borderline states. In *Psychoanalytic Psychiatry and Psychology,* ed. Knight and Friedman. New York: International Universities Press.

KNIGHT, R. P. Management and psychotherapy of the borderline schizophrenic patient. Ibid.

LITTLE, M. (1951). Countertransference and the patient's response to it. *Int. J. Psycho-Anal.,* 32.

MAHLER, M. S. (1968). *On Human Symbiosis and the Vicissitudes of Individuation.* New York: International Universities Press.

MAHLER, M. S. (1975). *The Psychological Birth of the Human Infant.* New York: Basic Books.

MASTERSON, J. F. (1972). *Treatment of the Borderline Adolescent: A Developmental Approach.* New York: John Wiley & Sons.

THE BORDERLINE ADULT 147

MASTERSON, J. F. The splitting defense mechanism of the borderline adolescent: Developmental and clinical aspects. In *Borderline States*, ed. J. Mack. New York: Grune & Stratton.

MASTERSON, J. F. (1976). *Psychotherapy of the Borderline Adult: A Developmental Approach.* New York: Brunner/Mazel.

MASTERSON, J. F. (1977). Primary anorexia nervosa in the borderline adolescent: an object relations view. In *Borderline Personality Disorders*, ed. Peter Hartocollis, M.D. New York: International Universities Press, pp. 475-494.

MASTERSON, J. F. (1978). Therapeutic alliance and transference. In *Amer. J. Psychiatry*, 135:4, 437-441.

MASTERSON, J. F. and RINSLEY, D. B. (1975). The borderline syndrome: The role of the mother in the genesis and psychic structure of the borderline personality. *Int. J. Psa.*, 56:163-178.

RINSLEY, D. B. (1977). An object relations view of borderline personality. In *Borderline Personality Disorders*, ed. Peter Hartocollis, M.D. New York: International Universities Press, pp. 47-70.

RINSLEY, D. B. (1974). Residential treatment of adolescents. In *American Handbook of Psychiatry*, ed S. Arieti. 2nd revised edition, Vol. II. New York: Basic Books, pp. 353-366.

ROSENFELD, H. (1958). Contribution to the discussion on variations in classical technique. *Int. J. Psycho-Anal.*, 39.

SEARLES, HAROLD F. (1967). Thought and thinking in the borderline state. *Psa. Review*, 53:4, 507-530.

SEARLES, HAROLD F. (1969). A case of borderline thought disorder. *Int. J. Psa.*, 50:655-664.

SEARLES, HAROLD F. (1977). Dual- and multiple-identity processes in borderline ego functioning. In *Borderline Personality Disorders*, ed. Peter Hartocollis. New York: International Universities Press, pp. 441-455.

SCHMIDEBERG, M. (1947). The treatment of psychopaths and borderline patients. *Amer. J. Psychotherapy*, 1.

SEGAL, H. (1964). *Introduction to the Work of Melanie Klein.* London: Heineman, and New York: Basic Books.

STERN, A. (1938). Psychoanalytic investigation of and therapy in the borderline group of neuroses. *Psychoanal. Quart.*, 7.

STERN, A. (1945). Psychoanalytic therapy in the borderline neuroses. *Psychoanal. Quart.*, 14.

WINNICOTT, D. W. (1965). *The Maturational Processes and the Facilitating Environment.* New York: International Universities Press.

ZETZEL, E. R. (1971). A developmental approach to the borderline patient. *Amer. J. Psych.*, 127:867-871.

Discussion

Dr. Searles: I am particularly interested in the ways in which Dr. Masterson's more global and objective stance, in conducting work with borderline patients or at least in conceptualizing such work, stands in contrast to my own relatively high degree of immersion in the feelings that one experiences in the course of this work. I should say, once again, that I found his paper highly instructive to me and I am necessarily, however, slanting my comments toward what I can say in the way of addition.

It is fair to say that Dr. Masterson reports to us extremely little of the feelings which the therapist experiences in doing this work, in much contrast to my own previously expressed views as to the degree in which the therapist or analyst necessarily shares in the therapeutic symbiosis with these patients, or at times feels himself a child threatened with abandonment by the patient as a mother, or feels threatened by the intensity of the patient's images of him as being an abandoning bad mother.

One of Dr. Masterson's few allusions to his own feelings

148

is when he says "patient *and therapist alike* [my italics] must learn to identify, endure, cope with and eventually resolve an apparent paradox. . . ." Early in his paper he says, as regards the consultations he has been doing with patients who have not been progressing in treatment with other analysts, "At first glance, one might suspect some of these were difficult or actually untreatable patients, or that the therapists either lacked adequate knowledge about therapy *or had such severe personal problems or such a countertransference that they were unable to conduct the treatment* [italics mine]." There is an emphasis that gives one to think that if one is feeling very much of, for example, rage at the patient, one is all too likely to have an unmanageable countertransference. He does acknowledge, as regards the working-through of the resistance, "it is an arduous task for the patient *and a trial of patience for the therapist* [italics mine]."

The firm but dispassionate stance which Dr. Masterson personifies and explicitly recommends throughout is shown in his statement that "the term confrontation is used not in the sense of the therapist's taking his aggression out on the patient or challenging him, but, rather, in the sense of bringing to the attention of the patient's observing ego the denied realistically destructive aspects of his defense mechanisms. . . . This stage can be stormy. . . ." This statement does not convey to me, however, the sense that the therapist ever is participating appreciably in the storminess, but only firmly and dispassionately coping with the storminess in the patient, and meanwhile avoiding even being challenging of or impatient with the patient.

My own criticisms of Dr. Masterson's main emphasis here are essentially three. First, I would be concerned that the therapist, in consciously maintaining such a stance, must inevitably be doing a great deal of projecting of his own more disturbed feelings of, for example, rage, abandonment-depression, and so on, on to the patient, so that the patient is essentially alone in having to deal with all the psychopathology in the relationship. Secondly, it seems to me that in order to more fully understand and theoretically conceptualize the nature of the psychoanalytic work with these patients, it is essential that a relatively full reporting of the therapist's subjective experience be included—all the more for the reason that so many of the patient's own unconscious feeling-experiences are first felt, in the course of the therapy, by the therapist on to whom the patient is projecting these feelings and attitudes. Thirdly, for relatively inexperienced therapists, it seems to me difficult for these relatively young persons to identify with the stance personified by Dr. Masterson, for he would have them feel, it seems to me, that if they are feeling intensely impatient with the borderline patient, or appreciably angry at him, or at all challenging of him, they are all too likely to be involved in an unmanageable countertransference, such that they should refer the patient to a more experienced and more dispassionate colleague.

Dr. Masterson says, "The borderline transference consists of the activation and alternate projection upon the therapist of the patient's primitive, split, positive and negative object relations part-units, which are then acted out in the transference." This statement, which so far as I know is unassailably true and well said, implies to me that the therapist inevitably will experience on innumerable occasions in his work with such a patient the patient's projected feeling experiences before the patient himself can become aware of them. Thus, the feelings that the therapist is having are of the very essence of what the treating of such a patient is about. Further, and in the same regard, it has been my experience in work with these persons that my own remarkably split images of any one patient, over the course of time, need to become integrated within myself before I can expect to help the patient to develop a better integrated, more coherent image of herself or himself.

Relatively late in his paper, Dr. Masterson is describing one patient's having acted out "the wish for reunion with me." One of the many things I miss in this paper are reports of the therapist's feeling of being in union with the patient, of coming to cherish that feeling of oneness with the patient, and coming to realize how much longing he himself can have for reunion with the patient. One gets the impression from this necessarily brief paper taken alone that Dr. Masterson does not at all experience himself at firsthand either the withdrawing object relations unit or the rewarding object relations unit emotions in the countertransference.

I reported in a recent paper (1976) something about my own as well as my patients' experiences of jealousy in the course of psychoanalytic therapy, and I wondered if Dr. Masterson were not reacting partly on the basis of quite understandable jealousy when he tells us about a part of his work with one of his male patients—the one about whom the lengthy vignette was given—wherein he is confronting the patient in regard to the latter's relationship with the patient's wife. "I confronted his clinging: I wondered why he was spending so much time with her, even having sexual intercourse, when his basic objective was to continue with the divorce. I pointed out that he was limiting her opportunities

for other relationships, as well as his own, and making it difficult for both of them to resolve their feelings about the
divorce." Moreover, to my mind, the underlying homosexual
transference material was developed further when Dr. Masterson tells us that the patient returned to the next interview
"with a full head of steam, in a rage at me for not giving him
the match." When the patient without warning wanted to cut
down the number of weekly sessions and Dr. Masterson interpreted this as an effort to lessen the pressure for individuation,
as well as to act out the anger in the transference for the frustration of the wish for unconditional love, the patient replied,
"You're like my parents, saying I can't do it except four times
a week, and I'm saying screw you, I'll show you. . . ."

This is something else I want to bring in. In my experience,
the more ill the patient with whom we are working is, the
earlier in his life history had he become the object of a transference from the mother or the father, or both, as being the
repersonification of the parent's own parents. Hence, for the
patient as a child, any prospect of his own becoming individuated in the setting of the family home was equivalent to
his own, as a transference parent to the mother for example,
abandoning her as his child (since he would be the abandoning mother toward his actual mother who has a transference
to him as being her mother). Similarly, for the mother of
such a child, toward whom she has an unconscious mother
transference, any prospects she herself may have of becoming
individuated have a connotation of her becoming liberated
from this transference parent of hers. That is, neither the
child nor the mother can differentiate between individuation
and a hostile abandonment of the other person, a hostile withdrawal from that person. And one of the aspects of working

with such people that I have tried to highlight in a recent paper (1978) has to do with the analyst as unwanted child. I come to realize that I'm being treated as an unwanted child.

I don't doubt, once again, that if Dr. Masterson's time had permitted he would have gone into a number of these areas, but I wanted to use the precious time I have to fill out some things to which his brief paper could not devote itself.

Dr. Kernberg: Dr. Searles has already said some of the things that I wanted to mention. Hearing you speak about this patient, I was struck by the fact that you called him Peter. I had to remind myself several times that this was not an adolescent but a 40-year-old man. Somehow you conveyed to me that he was a disturbed adolescent, rather than a grownup. I wondered whether that was part of a transference aspect—not taking him too seriously (in the sense of his being a grownup, responsible for his actions), in order to decrease the intensity of the transference-countertransference bind. Dr. Searles has commented on this extensively.

I would like to view this treatment from a different angle. Dr. Masterson said, "I wondered why he was spending so much time with her, with his wife, even having sexual intercourse, when his basic objective was to continue with the divorce. I pointed out that he was limiting her opportunity for other relationships as well as his own and making it difficult for both of them to resolve their feelings about the divorce." It seems to me that this comment does not fall within a position of technical neutrality. I found a superegoish aspect to it, and I was surprised because, usually, when relations break up, there is a lot of hatred and sex and love. I also wondered whether there was a premature deflection of the transference, by immediately referring the patient's present acting-out to its genetic origins in the past, without first fully exploring the negative transference development in the here and now. The danger is that patients learn rapidly about our own theoretical frames, they know what we are interested in and are only too happy to comply and give us our theories right back. I have sometimes felt that I am getting a caricature of my thinking from some of my patients, and it seems to me that the real test of whether or not theories conform to what we are observing is by exploring what is still unknown to both patients and ourselves—therefore, the unconscious aspects of the transference in the here and now must be explored fully.

In general terms, I had a certain sense that, although I theoretically agreed with both the application of a developmental viewpoint and an object relations viewpoint, the practical interventions seemed to somewhat oversimplify the kind of primitive object relations units activated in the transference. Dr. Masterson presented to us information indicating a possible combination of preoedipal and oedipal meanings of these part object relations units, so that his theoretical frame may be more restricted than the actual meanings of the units that were activated. And, if Dr. Searles is correct about the meanings of a homosexual transference that was also involved and not fully interpreted, then we might say that not only part object relations units were activated, but also, perhaps, more complex or advanced transference relationships, and that the transference did not reflect exclusively issues of separation-individuation. In short, I believe the complexities of the transference exceeded the relatively restrictive frame of reference that Dr. Masterson was using in this case.

Dr. Giovacchini: I don't know what I'm going to emphasize at this moment but I'm sure I've said it many times before. When I read this paper, I felt rather uneasy about it because I wanted to be critical of it and yet I couldn't think of anything I could concretely express. I believe I have been able to identify some of my uneasiness about it.

Of course, there are introjects within the ego of borderline cases. Within the ego, there are constricting introjects, maternal introjects, which crush the developmental potential. The aftereffects of traumatic experiences remain in the ego but not in the structured fashion Masterson describes. I have not encountered patients in whom these two units have been so graphically represented. They seem similar to a cartoon drawing where all of the subtle nuances are removed from the picture and you merely see an outline of the essentials. That such essentials exist I do not doubt, but that they manifest themselves in the therapeutic interaction in such a pure form I do doubt. I believe there is something about the egos, some lack of integration and structure at the points of fixation, of these patients that would not permit them to be able to integrate the experiencing of a rewarding or withholding mother.

Masterson postulates that the fixation of borderline patients occurs during the rapprochement phase of separation-individuation. A withdrawing or withholding mother would be experienced as a fairly sophisticated interaction. I believe that fixation occurs much earlier and that such an ego, one that uses splitting mechanisms, would not have achieved such a degree of separation. Masterson points out over and over again that the mother cannot separate herself from her child. The child can feel under these circumstances the pressure of intrusion or the pain of isolation, but not reward or abandonment which presupposes the capacity for clear-cut object relationships. Furthermore, in the same vein, I don't understand how the child and later adult can equate mother's abandonment with confidence. I don't think the feeling of confidence is compatible with borderline fixation. I believe it is compatible with depressive fixations. Masterson mentions a depressive element, and maybe he is addressing himself to that particular factor.

I was also struck by the fact that the patient is called Peter and he is 40 years old.

I also thought about how we project our theoretical orientations into the patient. I have one particular patient whom I have been seeing for many, many years. Once in a while he'll say, "Remember in 1968, you made the following interpretation?" I never made it, of course; I never had that kind of understanding about him, but I write it down and accept it. It's something I wish I had said.

I think there is an interesting point of focus among the three of us. Searles and Kernberg concentrate upon one particular clinical interaction and I do the same thing. So if you'll permit my formulation—it's not as flamboyant as homosexuality, and it's not as technical as Kernberg's, but let me throw it in because it represents my point of view which may or may not have anything to do with the patient. After

Masterson's remarks about the ex-wife and restricting her opportunities, the patient says, "I wish mother and everyone, even my ex-wife, could accept me as I am." Now I thought that "everyone," (I put a circle around everyone) was a direct reference to Masterson. In my mind, this was a transference response. The patient, in effect, was saying to Masterson, "Look, I wish you were interested in my welfare. I'm not concerned about what's going on with other people, I'm not paying you to worry about my ex-wife's welfare or what opportunities she's going to have." I felt that this was a rebuke of Masterson and this was carried to the next session with the incident of the matches and so on. I believe the matches and other items were displacements stemming from a reaction to the therapist that has transference elements. You see how different this formulation is. Masterson views the patient's reactions as diagnostic of the patient's immaturity, whereas I see them as artifacts caused by a judgmental confrontation, a response that was not dealt with.

Dr. Masterson: Dr. Searles, whose clinical perspective on the role of the therapist's feelings in psychotherapy is justifiably well-known and widely acclaimed, has distorted my perspective in order to create a straw man that he can demolish. We differ mainly in what importance to give countertransference in the overall therapeutic interaction. I have always included a careful evaluation of countertransference as *one* of the main factors to be considered. For example, my own countertransferencet in each phase of the therapy of the patient I described today was reported in another publication. In addition, as a supervisor I have long maintained that helping the resident with his countertransference frees him to learn from his patient. In sum, I have always viewed countertransference as *one* of the main factors to be considered.

Dr. Searles, on the other hand, views it as *the principal* if not the sole factor to be considered, i.e., "the feelings the therapist is having is the *essence* of what treating such a patient is all about." Beyond that, he states that the therapist who can maintain his therapeutic objectivity or neutrality must inevitably be projecting his own disturbed feelings on the patient. I disagree with both these assertions.

I think that, for the most part, it is possible to maintain an appropriate therapeutic objectivity which, however, is episodically interrupted by countertransference reactions which can be used as signals of the patient's projections. I think the therapist can observe and identify the patient's projections without necessarily having to react to them in his own feelings first. Finally, in my judgment, the notion that the maintenance of therapeutic objectivity requires the projection of disturbed feelings on the patient flies in the face of everything we have learned regarding personality development. The personality grows and matures through the resolution of conflicts at each stage of development, which results in a precipitate of intrapsychic structure. Despite the fact that the therapeutic relationship is a very special and intense one that evokes emotions that no other life situation would, I think the types and intensity of the feelings evoked will depend on how far the development of the therapist progressed and that if he has more or less successfully resolved his more primitive developmental conflicts, they have been transformed into intrapsychic structure and are therefore no longer available to appear in the countertransference except under extreme stress and regression.

Dr. Searles' third objection, that an objective therapeutic stance is difficult for residents to identify with—I presume he means to learn, again grossly distorts my point of view by implying that any countertransference feelings are inappropriate. Although it is, indeed, hard to learn therapeutic objectivity and countertransference feelings are inevitable, it seems to me vital that the young therapist learn, as much as possible, to distinguish between his feelings and his patient's feelings, between his emotional needs and his patient's therapeutic emotional needs. Moreover, I think Dr. Searles' perspective presents greater hazards to the young therapist. Dr. Searles is protected from therapeutically going astray as he immerses himself in and uses his own feelings by his extensive knowledge of personality development, psychopathology and therapy. The young therapist without these safeguards could be unduly vulnerable to going astray and using the therapy for his own emotional needs rather than those of the patient.

Dr. Searles' zeal in advancing his point of view is, to my mind, no better illustrated than his comment regarding jealousy and underlying homosexual transference material. His zeal causes him to fall into a trap that I'm sure rarely happens in his consulting room—i.e., using a transference interpretation without the conditions necessary for its effectiveness—i.e., a transference and free associations. For example, "a full head of steam" could just as easily be a metaphor for aggression as for sex.

To summarize, I think countertransference is one of many important variables in the therapeutic interaction. Its importance will vary from one treatment experience to the next and it is not always the sole or most important variable.

In replying to Dr. Kernberg, let me say that while I used the name "Peter" both to personify and to disguise the patient in the paper, in treatment I always referred to him by his last name.

The "super-egoish" aspects of the confrontation could result from the need to summarize the interaction. For example, the patient had been living for about a year with his girlfriend who, however, would not permit him to cling. Whenever a therapeutic confrontation evoked depression, he would depart from his usual routine and contact his ex-wife whom he may not have seen in weeks, have sexual relations with her, and then become overwhelmed with self-recrimination and remorse. My comment, which was basically a restatement of what he had been saying to himself, came only after many months of this behavior when I felt he was becoming ready to deal with his depression in his therapy.

It is difficult to know whether or not the transference was prematurely deflected. I couldn't agree more with Dr. Kernberg's comment that patients quickly learn our theories and use them for resistance so that we must exercise great caution in this regard. In general, my view is that if I do an appropriate job of confrontation, the patient will do the job of interpretation. I stick mainly with the transference feelings in the here and now and let the patient do the historical investigation as it emerges in his memories, dreams, etc.

I do not think this patient was intellectualizing as there was so much affect, so much content appropriate to affect, and so much resistance to both which, when dealt with, led to therapeutic progress. As to the quality of the transference exceeding the frame of reference, it seems to me that the homosexual elements in the transference emerge as the separation-individuation aspect of the problem is subsiding so that it is more a matter of timing than frame of reference. After all, this was not the presentation of a psychoanalysis, but the selection of one particular aspect to emphasize one issue.

Let me say to Dr. Giovacchini that the rewarding and withdrawing part-units are organizing abstractions derived from clinical material and therefore I don't think you could expect them to appear clinically in pure form. Their use allows us to look at the welter of clinical material in new and more meaningful ways. They also permit generalizations; however their use must not imply oversimplification in the sense of disregarding other important aspects of the clinical picture.

I can suggest several possible reasons why Dr. Giovacchini does not see this pattern in his patients. We all see mainly what we are accustomed to look for. This perspective differs from classical psychoanalytic theory (both instinctual and object relations) in that it organizes itself around the developmental process of separation-individuation within which it integrates both instinctual and object relations theory. This emphasis on separation-individuation is somewhat new and it always takes time to incorporate a new perspective. I feel sure that, given the opportunity, I could outline the pattern in the very patient Dr. Giovacchini presented today. The pattern, individuation—abandonment depression—defense, is so repetitive, so invariable, that I am surprised, in retrospect, that it went unnoticed for so long.

I don't think the child has to have a concept of the mother's withdrawal. This awareness only comes out in therapy after the defenses, such as splitting, have been overcome. The child only has to experience bad feelings as a result of one kind of interaction and good feelings as a result of another kind. In other words, the essential aspect does not take place at the cognitive level. Beyond that, the splitting defense mechanism would make it impossible for the child to formulate such a concept.

REFERENCES

SEARLES, H. F. (1976). Jealousy involving an internal object. Presented at the New York Conference on Borderline Disorders (under the auspices of Advanced Institute for Analytic Psychotherapy), New York City, Nov. 20, 1976.

SEARLES, H. F. (1978). (A) Jealousy involving an internal object, and (B) The countertransference in psychoanalytic therapy with borderline patients. To be published in *Stable Instability—Modern Approaches to the Borderline Syndrome*, ed. by Joseph LeBoit and Attilio Capponi. New York: Jason Aronson.

Index

Abandonment depression. *See* Depression

Acting-out, 32, 72. *See also* Working-through, transference acting-out
  control of, 31
  defined, 17
  focus in, 85
  and transference, 154
  and vacations, 61

"Adaptation to the 'Stronger' Person's Reality . . . of the Schizophrenic, The" (Stierlin), 49

Adler, G., on psychotherapy, 126, 146*n.*

Alienation:
  clinical material, 4ff.
  defensive adaptations, difficulties, 11ff.
  private reality, of patient, 9-11
  psychoanalytic treatment of, 3ff.

American Psychoanalytic Association, 107

Anal intercourse, 55

Apathetic terror, 67

"As-if" emotionality, 46

Autism, 44, 45, 68, 72
  and dependency, 24
  and development, 67-68
  in ego functioning, xi, 71

  term use, 67
  and twin, perception of, 53-54

"Autism and the Phase of Transition to Therapeutic Symbiosis" (Searles), 44

Autonomy:
  and boundary, 15-16
  and denial, 48

Avoidance, as defense, 32, 132

Balint, M., on ego growth, 88, 102*n.*

Bergeret, J., approach of, 93, 102*n.*

Berger, M. M., videotaping, 59, 63*n.*

Bibring, E., 102*n.*
  On ego psychology, 83
  on supportive psychotherapy, 80

Bion, W. R., on regression, 90, 102*n.*

Bipersonal field, 117

Bipersonal Field, The (Langs), 111

Borderline syndrome:
  defined, 71
  personality, 26ff.
  transference, 127ff.

Bowlby, John, 118

Brainwashing:
  desire for, 49
  and therapist, 69

Brody, W., on externalization, 11, 19*n.*

Castration anxiety, 127
Character neuroses, xi, 11ff.
  and adjustment, 11-12
  confusion on, 25-26
  and failure, 14-16
  and intersystemic conflict, 82
  meaning of, 30-32
  as threat, to therapist, 17-18
Chestnut Lodge 52, 72, 73
Clinging, 32, 132
Compulsion, and depression, 124
Countertransference, xi, 44, 60, 62.
    See also Transference.
  and acting-out, 96
  characteristics, 94
  denial of, 117
  idealization of, 70
  importance of, 157-60
  object relations in, 151
  and psychosis, 51, 52
  unmanageable, 149, 150
  and working-through, 125

Delusion, 16, 115
Denial, as defense, 32, 48, 130, 132
Depersonalization feelings, 144
Depression:
  and abandonment, 128-31, 133, 134,
    143, 144, 150, 161
  and compulsion, 124
  and confrontation, 160
  defense against, 30, 143, 144
  and suicidal fantasy, 140
Deutsch, Helene, on "as-if" emotional-
    ity, 46, 64n.
Diagnosis, of borderline, 114
Differential diagnosis, 24-25
Displacement:
  and therapist-patient, 132
  and transference, 157
Dissociation, and transference, 83
Downstate Psychiatric Institute, Di-
    rector of Training, 106
Dream analysis:
  abandonment fears, 141
  and alienation, 5-6
  emotional content, 60

value of, 69
Drug culture, 16
DSM diagnoses, I and II, 25

Easser, Ruth, on patients, 106
Ego. See also Ego psychology
  alliance of, 133
  boundaries of, 87
  and defense, 81
  dissolution of, 9
  fragmentation of, 47
  function of, 44
  identity of, 25
  integration of, 62
  mechanisms, and externalization, 10-
    11
  and object relations, 82
  pathology of, 137
  split, xii, 125, 127-31
  strengthening of, 91
Ego psychology, ix, x, xii, 78-79, 83,
    94, 101-102, 106, 108
Eisler, Kurt, on psychotherapy, 126,
    146n.
Electrocardiograms, 134
Empathy:
  capacity for, 70
  functions of, 91
  nature of, 92
  need for, therapeutic, 73
Expressive psychotherapy, 79, 85-86,
    110
Externalization, x-xi, 10-11, 22-23, 29-
    32, 37, 38, 72

Federn, P., on apathetic terror, 67, 73n.
Fixation:
  of ego, 128
  and narcissism, 13
  and psychosis, 86-87
  structure in, 155, 156
Free association, 49, 50, 140, 141
Freud, Sigmund. See also Psychoanal-
    ysis   on   acting-out/working-
    through, xii, 126-27, 146n.
  classic description of, 17
  on projection, 10, 19n.

Friedman, Henry J., on transference, 124, 146n.
Frosch, J., on psychotherapy, 123, 126, 146n.
"Function of the Patient's Realistic Perceptions . . . in Delusional Transference" (Searles), 47
Furer, M., approach of, 93, 102n.
Fusion:
 fantasy of, 29
 and hierarchy, 36

Gill, M. M. 102n.
 on ego psychology, 83
 on psychoanalysis, 78
Giovacchini, Peter L., xiii, 114, 161
 on alienation, 3ff., 34-39
 approach of, 93, 102n.
 on countertransference, 70
 discussed, 20ff.
 on discussion, 34-39
 interests of, x
 on Kernberg presentation, 107-109, 119
 on Masterson presentation, 155-57
 on psychotherapy, 123, 146n.
 on Searles presentation, 66-67
Grandiosity, in self-representation, 136
Green, André, approach of, 93, 102n.
Grinker, R. R., on supportive psychotherapy, 90, 102n.

Hartman, H., energic hypotheses, 109, 119n.
Hartocollis, P., approach summary, 94, 102n.
Hebephrenics, perception of analyst, 22. See also Schizophrenia
Heinmann, P., on psychotherapy, 123, 146n.
Homosexuality, 16, 156

Id:
 and defense, 81
 and object relations, 82
Identification:
 and acting-out, 61
 and analyst's feelings, 60

danger in, 59
 pathologic, 63
 of patient, with analyst, 61
Identity. See also Identification
 confusion in, 14-15, 69
 integration of, 114
Individuation, 44. See also Separation-individuation
 avoidance of, 130
 and ego, 137
 pressure of, 152
 term use, 67
Infantile psychosis, 46, 68
Introjects:
 in ego, 155
 and identification, 59
 and mother, 97

Kaplan, L., approach of, 93, 103n.
Kernberg, Otto F., xi, xiii, 73, 156, 160
 discussed, 35-37, 105ff.
 on discussion, 113-18
 on Giovacchini presentation, 24-28 146n.
 interests of, x
 on Masterson presentation, 153-55
 on object relations, 82, 83, 103n.
 on psychotherapy, 123, 126, 146n.
 on Searles presentation, 67-70
 technical approach, 88-90, 103n.
 on treatment approaches, 77ff.
Khan, M. M. R., on childhood, 47, 64n.
Klein, Melanie, 90, 109, 119n., 123, 146n.
Knight, R. P., on psychotherapy, 123, 146n.

Langs, Robert, 111-12
Lichtenstein, H., on symbiosis, 46, 64n.
Limit-setting, and interpretation, 38-39
Little, M.:
 on object relations, 89, 104n.
 on psychotherapy, 123, 146n.

Mahler, M., 90, 118
 approach of, 93, 103n.
 on autism, 67-68

on infantile psychosis, 46, 64n.
on mother-infant cuing, 59
on psychotherapy, 123, 146n.
on splitting, 88, 103n.
on symbiosis, 87, 103n.
Masochism, 4, 97
  for balance, 10
  motivations for, 28
Masterson, James F., xi, xiii, 108, 109,
    113, 114
  on acting-out/working-through,
    123ff.
  case report, 143, 147n.
  developmental perspective, 127, 128,
    147n.
  discussed, 37-39, 148ff.
  on discussion, 157-62
  on Giovacchini presentation, 29-34
  interests of, x
  on Kernberg presentation, 105-107,
    118
  on Searles presentation, 70-72
  on supportive psychotherapy, 92,
    93, 103n.
Masterson Group for the Study and
    Treatment of the Character Dis-
    orders, v
Megalomania:
  and delusion, 108
  expectations, 12
  intensity, 13
Myerson, P., on psychotherapy, 126,
    146n.

Narcissistic character, xi, 11-14
  confusion on, 25-27
  equilibrium in, 8, 15
  as patient, 30
  primary/secondary, 13
Nelson, Marie, paradigmatic psycho-
    therapy of, 52, 64n., 91, 103n.
Neurotics:
  competence of, 3
  reality testing, 114
Neutrality, technical, xii, 79-80, 84, 85,
    91, 106, 115
New Perspectives on Psychotherapy

of the Borderline Adult, con-
    ference on, ix
No and Yes: On the Genesis of Hu-
    man Communication (Spitz), 48
Nonverbal communication, 43, 69
Nursing infant, 48

Object relations, 81-83, 154
  British on, xii
  negative, part-units, 127
  split, xii, 127-30
  and split ego, 130-31
  and withdrawal, 136
  theory, 88-89, 93-95, 101
  and transference, 110
Oedipal conflict, 97, 101, 136-37
"One Day in the Life of Ivan Deni-
    sovich," 21
Oral dependency, 137

Paradigmatic psychotherapy, 52, 91
Paranoids:
  and antagonism, 57
  characteristics, 4
Passivity, 130
Projection, 32, 132, 136
  and analyst, 51-52, 61, 150
  and brainwashing, 49
  and child, 29
  of envy, 28
  and externalization, 10, 23
  of inadequacy feelings, 141
  paranoid, 144
  and part-units, 131-32
  and patient needs, 66, 67
  and therapeutic techniques, 91
Projective identification, 32, 92, 132
Psychoanalysis. See also Freud, Sig-
    mund
  classical model, 115, 123-24
  defined, 78, 116
  treatment, 77ff.
    alternative approaches, 89ff.
    approaches, 78-79
    case study, 97-102
    goals, 79
    and psychoanalysis proper, 84, 86

Psychoanalysis of Character (Giovac-
  chini), 33
*Psychoanalysis of Primitive Mental
  States* (Giovacchini), 35
Psychopharmacological treatment, 25

Regression, 130
  levels of, 87-89
  and primitivization, 35
  in psychoanalysis, 8
  and psychosis, 86-87
  rewarded, 128
  therapeutic, 90
Reichard, S., on structure, 17, 19*n*.
Repetition compulsion, 47, 126, 127
Repression, 77-78, 81, 114
Resistance, living through, 127
Rinsley, D., 147*n*.
  approach of, 93, 103*n*., 127, 128
  on psychotherapy, 123, 126
"Role of the Delusional Transference
  of the Patient's Realistic Perceptions of the Analyst, The"
  (Searles), 111
RORU, 133, 137, 143
Rosenfeld, H., on psychotherapy, 123,
  147*n*.

Sadism, and projection, 61
Sadomasochism, 4. *See also* Masochism
Scapegoating, of child, 29
Schizoid states, 47, 97, 108
Schizophrenia:
  and integration, 47
  perspective in, 52
  and reality testing, 114
  regressive features, 68
  and transference, 26
Schmideberg, M., on psychotherapy,
  123, 147*n*.
Schulz, Clarence G., 52
Searles, Harold F., xi, xiii, 26, 27, 93,
  94, 103*n*., 104*n*., 108, 116, 156-59
  on analyst, emotions, 153, 162*n*.
  on countertransference, 60, 64*n*.
  discussed, 35, 66ff.
  on discussion, 72-73

on ego functions, 44, 64*n*.
on Giovacchini presentation, 20-24
on homosexual transference, 154
interests of, x
on jealousy, patient, 15, 162*n*.
on Kernberg presentation, 109-13
on Masterson presentation, 148-53
on psychoanalysis, 43ff.
on psychotherapy, 123, 147*n*.
on schizophrenics, 87, 103*n*.
Seduction, and transference, 57-58
Segal, H., on psychotherapy, 123,
  147*n*.
Separation. *See also* Separation-individuation
  anxiety of, 131, 137
  term use, 67
Separation-individuation, 87-90, 125,
  128, 143, 144, 155, 161. *See also*
  Separation; Individuation
Spitz, R. A., 65*n*.
  on communication, 48
  on mother-infant cuing, 59
  on symbiosis, 50
Split ego. *See* Ego
Splitting, 32, 83, 132, 136, 162. *See also*
  Ego
Stern, A., on psychotherapy, 123, 147*n*.
Stierlin, Helm, on symbiosis, 49, 65*n*.
Structural organization, personality, 25
Submissiveness, and parental image, 82
Suicide:
  danger of, 107
  effect of, 59
  episodes, 144
  fantasy of, 140
  and team approach, 115
Superego:
  and aggression, 117
  and confrontation, 160
  and defense, 81
  and mother introject, 97, 99
  and object relations, 82
Supportive therapies, 78-80, 90, 92-93,
  114
Symbiosis:
  in development, 44-46, 87

and fusion, 26
preambivalent, 112
term use, 67

Technique, psychoanalytic therapy, 43ff.
Therapeutic alliance, 127, 131-32, 134
Therapeutic diagnosis, 36
Transference. *See also* Countertransference; Working-through, transference acting-out; Transference neurosis
    analysis of, xii, 28, 91, 92
    and analyst, 59-61
    of borderlines, 68
    case study, 96ff.
    and countertransference, 153
    delusional, 47
    and diagnosis, 36
    effect of, 116
    and expressive psychotherapy, 79
    focus on, 81, 84-85, 115
    function, 93
    and fusion, 33
    homosexual, 152, 154
    images in, 50-52
    importance of, 106
    and impulse/defense, 78
    interpretation, 38, 45, 159, 160
    and intrapsychic conflict, 83
    limitation, of, 30, 33
    of mother, 152
    negative, endurance, 20-22
    negative, origins, 154
    paradigms, 94, 110
    and past, reconstruction of, 27
    and psychosis, 26, 68, 124
    reactions, 112
    and regression, 26
    and repetition, 127
    and resistance, 79
    resolution of, 86
    response, 157
    and silence, 55-58

in supportive psychotherapy, 80
symbiotic, 25
and true analysis, 18
Transference acting-out. *See* Working-through, transference acting-out
Transference neurosis, regressive, 78, 84, 94, 116. *See also* Transference
Treatment approaches, borderline conditions, 77ff.

Videotaping, of analytic sessions, 58-59
Volkan, V., approach of, 93, 104*n*.

Winnicott, D. W.:
    case of, 38
    on coping, 131, 147*n*.
    on diagnosis, 36, 39*n*., 123, 147*n*.
    on growth, 88
    on object relations, 89, 104*n*.
    on psychotherapy, 123, 147*n*.
    on separation-individuation, 87, 104*n*.
Withdrawing Object Relations Unit (WORU), 132, 134, 136, 138, 143, 145
Wolberg, Arlene, projective techniques of, 91, 104*n*.
Working-through, transference acting-out, xii, 123ff. *See also* Acting-out; Transference
    borderline transference, 127ff.
    discussion, 143-45
    Freud on, 126-27
    management, case study, 134ff.
    phase of, stuck in, 125
    psychotherapy, 132-34
    split ego, 128-31
    split object relations, 127-31
    therapeutic alliance, 131-32

Zetzel, E. R., on psychotherapy, 90, 104*n*., 123, 147*n*.